T0209425

THEY CALL

TISHOMINGO COUNTY

HOME

Betty Compton

BALBOA.PRESS

A DIVISION OF HAY HOUSE

Balboa Press books may be ordered through booksellers or by contacting:

Balboa Press
A Division of Hay House
1663 Liberty Drive
Bloomington, IN 47403
www.balboapress.com
1 (877) 407-4847

Because of the dynamic nature of the Internet, any web addresses or links contained in this book may have changed since publication and may no longer be valid. The views expressed in this work are solely those of the author and do not necessarily reflect the views of the publisher, and the publisher hereby disclaims any responsibility for them.

The author of this book does not dispense medical advice or prescribe the use of any technique as a form of treatment for physical, emotional, or medical problems without the advice of a physician, either directly or indirectly. The intent of the author is only to offer information of a general nature to help you in your quest for emotional and spiritual well-being. In the event you use any of the information in this book for yourself, which is your constitutional right, the author and the publisher assume no responsibility for your actions.

Print information available on the last page.

ISBN: 978-1-9822-4293-0 (sc)
ISBN: 978-1-9822-4295-4 (hc)
ISBN: 978-1-9822-4294-7 (e)

Library of Congress Control Number: 2020902911

Balboa Press rev. date: 03/25/2020

CONTENTS

Chapter 1   Land Between the Creeks 1

Chapter 2   Anna Brown - Old Tishomingo County 7

Chapter 3   Crawford - Eastport the River Town 15

                  Bugg Family - Short, Mississippi 17

Chapter 4   Osborn Family - Hubbard Salem 27

                  Grisham Family - Red Sulfur Road 31

Chapter 5   Compton - The Railroad brings family to Burnsville... 49

Chapter 6   The Brumley Family - Sardis Road 77

                  The Mann family - Big Baby Jones Hill 86

Chapter 7   Osborn Family - The Powhatan 93

Chapter 8   Rachel's Family 103

Chapter 9   Skirmishes at Glendale and Burnsville 109

Chapter 10 The Marlar - Cummings - Lambert Family 123

Chapter 11 The Welch family - Eastport 139

                  At Home in Iuka 146

Chapter 12 Researching your Roots 155

STORIES

Singing Hatchet Women 2

Hubbard Cemetery 10

The Panther 14

The Baby Blues 23

The Horse thief 25

Chicken and Dumplings 29

Tom's Smoke House and Corn Crib 34

Pass the sweet potatoes 37

Lee bell's mule 38

The Baptism 52

A Mail Order Bride 53

The Quakers 56

The Happy Hollow Ghost 61

World War II 70

The Cow Boy 72

Honky Tonk City 74

Grandpa's New Wife 88

The Indian Princess 94

Extracting the Pea 101

Iuka Drive-In 105

We got married in a snow storm 107

The Rooster Fighter 129

The Lambert, Marlar Feud 131

The Meanest Town in Mississippi 134

The Gunboats 141

The Thanksgiving Squirrel 147

Charley, the Catfish 150

The Trotline 152

The Hillbilly Spa 157

Dousing for Graves 159

Tishomingo County Families

Crawford
Bugg
Brown
Palmer
Osborn
Compton
Seaton
Fields
Mann
Brumley
Handley
Welch
Marlar
Hubbard
Cummings
Lambert

This book is a combined study of genealogy, history, and family literature.

Old family stories paint a vivid description of people and their way of life. They have been passed by word of mouth through several generations. All are pulled from the memories of a long forgotten past.

I hope to pass these stories on to you, just the way they were told to me. I cherish so many who have welcomed me into their homes and shared these echoes of the past.

I also want to pass on the awe and admiration I have for these people. They lived through every historical event that shaped Tishomingo County. A strong people, they built a place for their children that our generation can be proud to call home.

My research is limited to an area of northern Tishomingo County. The land that borders the Tennessee River, between Yellow Creek and Bear Creek. It also reflects the history of these hometowns - Iuka, Eastport, Burnsville, and Short.

CHAPTER 1

LAND BETWEEN THE CREEKS

The first child in our family to be born in Tishomingo County was Indiana Victoria Bugg, Born in Short, Mississippi in 1844, she married Robert Taylor Brown, and was known as Anna Brown.

The waterfalls near Short were located on her land. Some of her family have lived here since 1833. They were some of the first settlers in this area. Water flowed over these falls long before Pickwick Lake was formed. Before they were the Anna Brown Falls, they had an Indian name. Bokoshi was the Chickasaw word for river. Before 1837, this was the homeland of the Chickasaws.

Some of the first written history of this area was recorded in 1540. Hernando Desoto is thought to have discovered the Tennessee River in present day Tishomingo County. Although he is better known for discovering the Mississippi river. He learned of the big river from the Chickasaw people that lived here. The explorer changed his route and traveled south to present day Tupelo. There he spent the winter at a large village called Ackia.

The Tennessee River derives its name from the Cherokee village of "Tanasi". On a 1755 British map it is referred to as "The River of the Cherokees."

Descendants of Anna Brown saw signs of the people that inhabited the land before them. Many locations have Indian names. The Bugg children played on an Indian mound that was on a ridge above the river. They also hunted arrow heads on a hill where flint weapons and tools were made. It is the present site of the JP Coleman Park Lodge.

In the 1700's several villages along Big Bear Creek could not be identified as Cherokee or Chickasaw. This land is near the border of the two Nations.

By 1765, the Chickasaws built villages along Big Bear Creek (Ocochappo). There is much written about the mouth of Bear Creek. Many traveled a Chickasaw trail that crossed the river here. This site would later become Eastport, Mississippi and Riverton, Alabama.

"Singing Hatchet Women"

For many years the Chickasaws were at war. A small nation, they had to defend their land against larger tribes. They became strong warriors and were known as a fierce people. Not many dared to settle their land.

Education began early in their culture. Training to sharpen their skills began as toddlers. Boys were given toy weapons. Girls were given baskets and pottery to make. By the time children were teenagers, they knew how to go into battle or take care of a household. Not every one was a warrior, but each one had a job to do.

An English trader, traveling through Indian lands, witnessed some of their tactics.

War cries sounded as fighting began. Women warriors were singing from the trees. Words that were meant to put fear into the heart of the enemy.

"We are going to kill you! But first we will torture you!" OOOOOOOO EEEEEEEE OOOOOOOO EEEEEEEE

The singers warned the braves of dangers. "Ambush" They directed the fighting with their songs. "Retreat Attack" Defeat of their enemies came quickly.

Armed with hatchets, the women were ready to join the fight, if needed. The warriors, both men and women, instilled fear into their enemies.

In the early 1800's, some of the English traders married Chickasaw women.

The Colbert Brothers, as well as other half breeds became the tribe leaders, signing treaties and dealing with the government. They spoke the language of the English and the Chickasaws.

Levi Colbert owned a ferry and travelers inn at the mouth of Bear Creek until 1802. In this treaty, the Natchez Trace was moved from Bear Creek to Colbert County, Alabama. Levi Colbert moved his ferry up the river. The Colbert's lived on large Plantations. They owned many slaves that operated the farms, ferry boats, and cotton gins.

Under the Colbert leadership, the Chickasaws became a wealthy nation. Only natives could own and operate a business on their land. Before 1837, they owned towns with stores, mills, cotton gins and black smith shops. Many plantations raised thoroughbred horses.

LaDonna Brown shared information about her family. My fifth great grandfather was Wilson Frazier. Government records state he was a full-blooded Chickasaw plantation owner. He lived on the east side of the Tombigbee River. His family left in November of 1837 and came to Indian Territory.

My mom's people are from the Raccoon Clan. They are known to come from the peace town or white town. The Battle of Hikkya, otherwise known as Ackia was fought here. My fifth great grandfather's name was Jesse Brown. It is interesting to note that by the time of the removal, both of my grandfathers had English names. My grandmothers didn't.

Chickasaw lands before treaties were signed.

Land was ceded to the US Government in Treaties signed in 1805, 1816, 1818, and 1832.

The treaty of 1832 included lands from Alabama to the Mississippi River. This treaty included Tishomingo County. All the other treaties were of hunting grounds or land they had gained in battle. This was their homeland. It took from 1832 to 1837 for the Chickasaws to relocate to Oklahoma.

Tishomingo County was formed Feb. 9, 1836. The land ceded in the treaty of 1832 by the Chickasaws would be divided into 10 counties - Tishomingo, Tippah, Marshall, Desota, Tunica, Panola, Fayette, Pontotoc, Itawamba, and Chickasaw.

Tishomingo contained 923,040 acres of land. Often referred to as "The state of Tishomingo" because of its size. It included the present counties of Prentiss, Alcorn and Tishomingo.

The word Tishomingo means "Warrior Chief". The largest county was named after the last war chief of the Chickasaws.

The land across the river in Alabama, and Tennessee was settled 16 years before land in Tishomingo County. Nearby Waterloo, Ala. was populated enough to be incorporated as a town in 1832.

The river landings that would become Short and Eastport, had some early settlement because of river travel. A few settled along the river as early as 1833.

Most of Tishomingo county was not settled until after 1837. At that time the largest migration of settlers in the country began. A million acres of land was sold by the government in one years time.

CHAPTER 2

ANNA BROWN - OLD TISHOMINGO COUNTY

The Bugg family, like many early settlers traveled down the Tennessee River to settle along the creeks. Waterways were the only roads in this area except for the Natchez Trace.

Thomas Jefferson Bugg and his wife, Amelia Victoria Crawford, (Millie Bugg) moved to Mississippi from Talbotton, Georgia between 1833 and 1837. They came about the same time the new county was formed.

The trail they took to come to the Mississippi Territory from Georgia was traveled on land and water. By horse drawn wagons, they traveled an old Indian trail from Augusta to Chattanooga. Here they boarded a flat boat on the Tennessee River that carried them to Muscle Shoals, Alabama. After unloading at the shoals, their next stop was Waterloo, Ala. which was located eight miles west of the shoals. Here they boarded boats that took them six miles down river. The area they settled was called Short.

Amelia and Thomas were born on cotton plantations. They were married 19, November 1823. Several generations of the Bugg and

Crawford family lived near Augusta, Georgia. The land they lived on was acquired by their Grandfather. It was land that opened up for settlement after the Revolutionary War.

Charles Crawford was the first Crawford to settle in Georgia. He along with three of his sons, received land grants, because of their service in the revolutionary war. He was from Virginia. Most of Amelia's family stayed in Georgia. Because of these large land grants, they owned plantations in Crawford and Appling, Georgia.

The Buggs also had several generations that lived in Georgia. Jacob Bugg was the first to come to Georgia from Virginia. Amelia and Thomas Bugg brought five children to the Mississippi territory.

Sarah Victoria Bugg b.1824
Lycurges Gearldine Bugg b. 1828
Amelia Louisa Jane Bugg b. 1829
Caroline Evaline Amelia Bugg b.1830
Syderham Albinous Bugg b.1832

Sarah Bugg married George Washington Tackett. She lived in Eastport in 1850 and 1860. 1870 she lived in Short, next door to her brother Lycurges. Sarah died in Iuka Mississippi in 1887.

Lycurges Bugg married Mary Ann Walker in 1850 in Iuka, Mississippi. He lived in Eastport in 1850 and in 1860. In 1870 and 1889 his residence was Short, Mississippi.

Lycurges and Mary Bugg are buried in the Hubbard Family Cemetery. Descendant's that carry the Bugg name came from Lycurges, and his brother, Syderham Bugg.

Lycurges Gearldine Bugg

Louisa Bugg married Seaborn T. Moore in 1851. Sadly he died only a few months after they married. In 1852 she married Bill Peel in Tishomingo Co. In 1868 she married Bluford Clinton Reynolds in Alcorn Co. Louisa died in Colin Texas in 1896. She is buried there with two of her husbands. She was the only child of Thomas Jefferson and Amelia Bugg to leave Tishomingo County. Louisa's youngest son is buried in the Hubbard Cemetery. She had children by all three of her husbands.

Caroline Bugg married Green Finley Hubbard. She lived in Eastport in 1850 and in 1860. In 1870 and 1880 she lived in Short Ms. She died in 1904. Green Finley and Caroline Hubbard are buried in the Hubbard Family Cemetery, which is located in the yard of their home. It is also within one half mile of the waterfalls.

Syderham Bugg married Nancy E. Johnson in 1869. In 1850 Syd lived in Eastport in 1850. By 1870 and 1880, he lived in the Short Miss. area. Syd and Nancy Bugg are buried in the Johnson Cemetery, which is located north of the Hubbard family Cemetery. It is also located on a ridge above the river.

Indiana Bugg was born in Short, Ms. in 1844. She was the youngest child, and the only child born in Mississippi. Her father, Thomas Jefferson Bugg died when Indiana was a baby. The last record I have of him is in 1845. His burial place is unknown, although he died while living in the first settlement of Short Miss.

Amelia Bugg's burial place is also unknown. She died in Short, while living in the home of her daughter, Indiana Brown. Her death was in 1880, at the age of 76. Thomas died thirty-two years before the oldest marked tombstone in the Hubbard Family Cemetery. So, he died before the cemetery was started.

"Hubbard Cemetery"

When I was a small girl, around 1958, I went to the Hubbard Cemetery with Mrs. Jeanie Johnson (Lou Genia Hubbard). She cleaned off the graves and told me about some of the people buried there.

First was her mother, Susie Hubbard, her father, Robert Lee Hubbard, and five of their children. Four died at an early age. Her brother lived to be a young man. He was shot and killed in a fight at Red Sulfur Springs in Hardin Co. Tenn. Her father, Robert Lee Hubbard, everyone called him Bob, got life in prison. He shot and killed an innocent man. Sadly, He thought he was shooting the man that killed his son.

She showed me the grave of a young black boy. Nobody knew who he was. Her father found him floating in the river at Bugg Landing. He pulled him out. Later he came back with his wagon and brought him up the hill to Hubbard Cemetery. Genie was a young child at the time, around 1902. She remembers her dad saying they were going to give him a proper burial. A few people from the community sang hymns, read from the Bible, and prayed for his soul. They marked his grave with a rock.

Miss Jeanie showed me the grave of her grandparents, Caroline Bugg and Green Finley Hubbard. Her grandmother's brother, Lycurges Bugg was buried here with many of his family.

She also showed me the grave of a family friend who committed suicide. He came to this tragic end because he spent all of his children's inheritance. When the time came to give them the money, he couldn't face them. Using a sharp fork, he cut his wrist and bled to death.

Lee Osborn's family lived in that same house after he died. His wife said that every time it rained, dark stains came up on the wooden floor, where he bled to death. She used everything she could think of to clean them. Buttermilk and turpentine should clean any stain. They would disappear until it rained again!

The oldest marked tombstone in Hubbard Cemetery is 1877. There are 14 graves that are only marked with a rock. There are several other unmarked graves. Some they didn't know were there until they dug into them. Many of the early graves did not have markers.

Bert Bugg told about fourteen children that are buried there. They died of the bubonic plague in Riverton and Waterloo. These unmarked graves are on the outer edge of the cemetery.

Amelia Bugg's grandchildren tell about a story they heard as children. The oldest building in Short, was a log cabin located at the end of Bugg Landing (Whetstone Hollow). Four of Amelia Bugg's brothers built the cabin as a hunting lodge. They were from Columbia Co. Georgia, near Augusta. Family stories have the Crawford brothers owning thousands of acres of land in this area. They had hunting lodges where Waterloo, Coleman Park, and Short are located today. Some think the brother's may have leased land from the Indians to hunt on. This would have been in the early 1830's. The brother's never lived here. Amelia's youngest brother, Milton Crawford owned a plantation in Aberdeen Miss. He lived there in 1840. Amelia was the only child in the Crawford family that made this area her home.

The earliest deed I found for Thomas Jefferson Bugg, was for five acres to Milton Crawford and Thomas Jefferson Bugg. It was made in 1839. They owned the land at Bugg Landing along Whetstone creek.

In 1852 Milton Crawford deeded as gifts, 260 acres of land to Amelia Bugg and her six children. He divided it evenly into 7 lots. The land lay along Whetstone Creek and along the Tennessee River. Sections 31and 32, Township one, Range 11E. They inherited their father's part of the land. Thomas Jefferson Bugg, and Amelia's brothers bought 589 acres of land in 1839. These lots have belonged to the Bugg children's descendants since 1852.

Lot 1 - Sarah Bugg
Lot 2 - Amelia Bugg
Lot 3 - Louisa Bugg
Lot 4 - Syderham Bugg
Lot 5 - Indiana Bugg
Lot 6 - Caroline Bugg Hubbard
Lot 7 - Lycurges

The Old Bugg Homeplace

Amelia Louisa Jane Bugg Reynolds
Abel Walker Bugg
Indiana Victoria Bugg Brown (Anna Brown)
Ludy Reynolds and Anna Brown were sisters

"The Panther"

One night, a descendant's wife, and a small boy were in the hunting lodge alone. They were attacked by a panther. They said it scratched the door trying to get into the cabin. The attack lasted all night. The woman cut up all the furniture in the house. She burned it in the fireplace to keep the panther from coming down the chimney on them. The only thing that saved them was daylight.

After the husband came home, they tracked the animal with dogs, and killed it. It was said to stretch out 7 feet long. Bert Bugg took the cabin door and put it in his barn. Grandkids remember seeing the scratches on the door. The log cabin rotted and fell down many years ago.

That's not the only story I heard about Panthers at Hubbard Salem. When Rachel Mann was a small child, her grandmother was picking walnuts at a tree, across from Hubbard Salem Church. It was almost dark. Grandma Mann and Rachel were baking a cake for Sunday dinner. All at once they heard a terrible loud scream! It almost sounded human! Grandma Mann grabbed Rachel and ran to their log cabin. She closed all the shutters on the windows. They didn't have glass windows. She said, "That's a panther! They've been known to kill folks in these parts."

CHAPTER 3

CRAWFORD - EASTPORT
THE RIVER TOWN

After Thomas's death in 1845, Amelia and her children moved from Short to District 4 in Eastport, which was about four miles away. The original Eastport lay along the river bottom only three miles north of Cook's Landing.

Eastport was a Chickasaw Indian post before 1832. It was also the point where the Natchez Trace crossed the Tennessee River at the mouth of Bear Creek. Indians had traveled through this area for over one hundred years. The Chickasaw Indians gave an easement to allow travelers to pass through their nation on the Natchez Trace in 1801. The route where the Natchez Trace crossed the Tennessee River changed from Bear Creek to Colbert Co. in 1802.

Eastport was a thriving town with over 2,000 residents in 1850. Large riverboats docked there. They brought merchandise in and they shipped it out to other parts of the country. Farmers came from all over old tishomingo county to sell their crops and goods. Riverboat trade made Eastport a wealthy town.

It was the largest settlement in Tishomingo County. It was also the gateway for settlers to come and buy land. Many wagon trains stopped here.

All roads led to Eastport. River trade made Tishomingo one of the richest counties in the state.

A bridge that spanned two hundred feet crossed Bear Creek and connected Eastport with Riverton. In the years before 1862, residents used this bridge to travel to Alabama. Waterloo and Eastport were well connected by water and by land.

Indiana spent her childhood in Eastport. Amelia and the Bugg children lived there for fifteen to twenty years, during Eastport's peak years. In the 1850 census, their house number was 1059. Amelia's children moved out as they married and made homes of their own. But they continued to live in Eastport until after 1860.

Once a year, the Bugg Family would pack some food, such as (biscuits, fried meat, boiled eggs, fried dried apple pies, baked sweet potatoes). They would travel to Jacinto in their wagons, which were pulled by a pair of horses. People went to Jacinto to pay their taxes. It was the County seat. The trip from Eastport to Jacinto took three days. The family slept in their wagons along the way. Hotels were available once they got there.

There were two roads to Jacinto from their part of the county in 1860. The first road went from Eastport, Iuka, Cartersville, and on to Jacinto. The second road left Neshoba, Farmington, and on to Jacinto. Neshoba was a former Indian village located near the mouth of Yellow Creek where it emptied into the Tennessee River. Taxes were paid at Jacinto from 1836 until 1870 when Alcorn County was formed and the County seat of Tishomingo County became Iuka.

Indiana and Amelia still lived in Eastport in 1860. They lived in the same location as Lycurges Bugg and his family, household 2807. Amelia Moore lived with her Grandmother Amelia that year. She was the daughter of Indiana's sister Louise and her first husband Seaborn Moore.

Amelia's property was worth $3,000 on the 1860 census of Eastport. She lived next door to two of her daughters, their property was valued at $100. Sarah and her husband George Tackett lived with their children in household 2806. Caroline and her husband, Green Finley Hubbard lived with their children in household 2809.

Bugg Family - Short, Mississippi

Sometime after the 1860 census, the Bugg family moved back to Short Miss. There were probably more than one reason they moved. Amelia and her son's were listed as farmers in Eastport. They farmed the rich river bottom lands. This area flooded often.

The Memphis Charleston Railroad began construction in 1852. The first railroad in Tishomingo County began at Memphis, Tennessee and Stevenson, Alabama. The last spike was driven just outside the Iuka city limits on April 1857. It was finished five years after it began. The towns of Eastport and Farmington were abandoned. River trade practically shut down. Railroad towns like Corinth, Burnsville, and Iuka saw rapid growth. The railroad changed the way of life in Tishomingo County. Store bought clothing and merchandise became accessible. General Merchandise Stores opened up in all towns.

The civil war started in 1860. There was heavy fighting in Eastport in April 1862. Union Gunboats shelled the town. All of the residents were forced to leave their homes. The town of Eastport did not rebuild and it ceased to exist as a town after 1870.

By 1860, Corinth took Eastport's place as the largest town in Tishomingo County. It grew because two railroads crossed here.

The Bugg family moved four miles down the river. They returned to Short. In 1852, their Uncle Milton Crawford deeded 240 acres of land on a ridge above the Tennessee River. It was an inheritance from their father, Thomas Jefferson Bugg. They built homes on this land sometime after 1860. That was the last year they were on the Eastport census.

The first post office of Short, Miss. was located on the north side of the road, across from the Hubbard Family Cemetery. The Green Finley Hubbard and Caroline Bugg Hubbard family home place was located near the post office. Many Hubbards were born in this house. Rachel Mann and Dick Bullard, Indiana's great grand children were born here. It later belonged to Evelyn Jourdan, a Hubbard Granddaughter. She remodeled the old home. The house burned in the 1960's.

A school was built in short after the civil war. It was located near the waterfalls. The students called it "Hog College". They probably called it that because it was an agricultural school. Students attended this school in the 1870's through the 1900's. In 1903 the school was moved to the Hubbard Salem Church. In the 1940's the Hubbard Salem students were moved to Central School and Iuka High School.

Clyde Grisham, (some called him A.C. Grisham) was a post master there. People would come in to Bugg Landing and walk a short distance, up the hill, to Short. Bugg Landing is Whetstone Hollow today. It is the next hollow north of the Falls.

In the 1800's the river ran close to the bank on the Mississippi side near Bugg Landing and at the Falls. The hollow was deeper and longer. It was a good place to land boats.

Before Eastport was built, riverboats would stop at Short. People would turn their orders in and goods would be shipped to Short from Paducah, Kentucky. Boats would dock and blow their horn. People met the boats and loaded the goods they ordered.

After Eastport became a big port, they had to go there to pick up their orders. They traveled on a road that went along the river from Short to Eastport.

The roads around Short followed the hollows. It was hard to climb the hills with wagons. Four roads that ran along the river at Short, connected at the Hubbard Salem Church.

Short, Ms. changed locations several times. It started at Bugg Landing, when river travel was the only road into this area. This early river settlement of Short, Ms. was one of the earliest settlements in Tishomingo County. The Bugg family lived in the river settlement of Short from 1833 until 1845 when they moved to Eastport. Eastport may have moved to them. It was less than four miles from Short. Eastport started to grow and expand along the river.

The second location of Short moved off the river to the top of the hill. This is in the location of the Hubbard Family Cemetery and the first Short, Ms. post office.

In the 1870's Cook's Landing became the prominent port and settlement moved to that area. When Hubbard Salem Church was built in the 1880's many homes went up near the church. The school at Short was moved to Hubbard Salem Church in 1903. That's another reason the name changed from Short to Hubbard Salem. The Red Sulfur Road also drew settlement. All of these areas were known as Short, Ms.

In the 1930's, Short was located at the 4 way stop where you turn to go to Coleman Park. The Post Office was relocated from the Hubbard Family Cemetery area, to Julian Busby's store. After the post office moved the old area of Short became Hubbard Salem.

Red Sulfur Road went through Short. It was the main highway that connected Tishomingo County, Ms. and Hardin County, Tn. In later years, residents crossed the steel bridge and traveled to Hardin County Tenn. Red Sulfur Springs, Hardin County Tennessee was close enough to get to by foot. Some of the boys that were seeing girls in Hardin County, walked to see them, especially on Sunday afternoons.

One Sunday before the steel bridge was built, Ben Osborn rowed his boat across yellow creek. He was going to visit a girl that lived on the hill above Red Sulfur Springs near Shangai Church. A storm came up and the creek was too rough to cross. In that day and time, it was not proper for a young man to stay at the girl's house. He visited Mrs. Morris. She was an elderly widow that lived near the crossing. She was known to let stranded travelers stay at her house. She was also kin to most of the people that lived across the river. Ben's family had no way of contacting him. They hoped he was waiting out the storm. It was two days before the water was calm enough to cross.

Yellow Creek was wide enough for steamboats when the water was high. They came off the Tennessee River, up Yellow Creek for a short distance, and docked at Zippy Creek. Today, Zippy Creek is located across the river from Grand Harbor Marina. It was named after Zeporrah Johnson, who along with her sister, Salina Johnson, ran a boarding house. Most of her customers were steamboat passengers.

The Johnson sisters were considered to be wealthy. They had more money than most of their neighbors. They did not trust banks, so they buried their money in fruit jars. Many treasure seekers still dig around the sister's home place with hopes of finding their money.

James Bond's grandmother said the Johnson sisters told her they buried their money where they could see it from the barn, while they were milking and from the front porch. It was in their sight most of the time.

In the early 1900's, big boats docked at Cook's Landing. People walked up the hill to Short. They would cross the river, and go to Waterloo, Ala. In 1870 there was a large sawmill located at Cook's Landing. It was said that it supplied the lumber that built Eastport. In 1870 and 1880, this area was being settled and developed.

The community of Short grew along the Red Sulfur Road. Short had several stores, physicians, houses, and churches. That big sawmill at Cook's Landing supported the lumber business. Boats bringing in supplies and passengers also brought business to the town. They had a Boarding House. People came from all over the area to buy supplies at Cook's Landing.

Annie Osborn Mann, Indiana's granddaughter told about her husband, Jessie Lee Mann, teaching adult education in the Short Post Office. This was about 1935. He taught adults to write their name, figure their crops, and exchange money. He also taught school at Short Creek, a nearby settlement that had their own school and community.

In 1935, TVA was clearing the land around yellow creek to build Pickwick Dam and Pickwick Lake. TVA's Family Survey for removal and relocation gave a lot of information about the people that lived in this area.

Lee Osborn's case file stated he had been hired by TVA to help clear the land around Yellow Creek. He was working there on October 1935 the day of the survey. His salary was $360.00 a month. A family of three lived in an unpainted wooden structure with a fireplace for heat, oil lamps for light, and a spring as their source of water. Lee's home was typical of many homes in the area except most families were larger than three.

Andrew Morris also lived on yellow creek. His survey stated ten people lived in his house. He had wood heat, oil lamps, and a spring for water. His household also had a sewing machine. Sam Osborn's survey showed a similar household, except he had a well. These homes were typical of all the other homes in the area.

This settlement of Short, which started around the 1860's was a thriving settlement until Pickwick Lake was formed in 1939. Hubbard Salem, (the old Short Ms. area) was now on a peninsula that was isolated from Eastport, Lauderdale and Hardin County by Pickwick Lake. The economy of Short, Ms. failed. Many business owners, as well as residents moved to nearby Iuka, Ms.

Jessie Lee Mann

Annie Osborn Mann

"The Baby Blues"

Annie Mann told about a terrible experience she had, while living in Hubbard Salem.

Her second child, Ollie Ruth Mann, was born in 1936. Jessie Lee, her husband went for the doctor, as soon as they knew the baby was coming. He was one of the few people in that area that had a car. If anyone got hurt, they asked him to take them to the doctor. He was used to hunting the doctor. Annie said, "The baby's coming! Go get Tom Grisham!" Tom had helped birth his own children. Tom clamped the cord and cut it. The baby and mother seemed to be doing fine!

That night the doctor was not at home. Jessie went all around the neighborhood looking for him. Finally someone told him that the doctor was coon hunting. Jessie went to several places that they usually hunted. By the time the doctor got there, the baby was six hours old. The doctor said the cord was too long, so he recut it.

At first Ollie Ruth seemed to be healthy. But her navel didn't heal. It ruptured. Ollie Ruth, only lived 2 months.

Annie's family thought she was going to die from grief. Her arms throbbed with pain, just to hold Ollie Ruth. Annie went through different stages of insanity. Jessie never left her alone, he followed her to Hubbard Salem Cemetery. There she questioned, "How God could let this happen?" Nothing anyone said could comfort her. Watching her baby suffer and die drove her crazy!

Next she blamed the doctor. She hated him!!! She planned how she would go to his house, call him out, and shoot him. Again Jessie tried to comfort her. He told her, "Annie, the doctor did everything he knew to do. He was trying to help Ollie Ruth. We can't blame him." She thought, "If I shoot him I'll probably go to hell and I'll never get to see my baby, because I know she's in Heaven." "They will put me in prison and I want get to be with my other child." "Oh, How I want to kill him, but I can't."

Ok, if she couldn't blame the doctor or God. The only person left to blame was herself. Annie quit eating. She quit talking. She lay with her eyes closed and wished herself dead. She constantly heard her baby crying! The feeling that she couldn't do anything to help her, never went away.

Annie not only detested herself, she couldn't stand her husband, either. How he could forgive so easily, and go to work every day, just like nothing had happened!

Grandma Mann knew Annie was in a serious condition. Her thoughts went back to a scene on Indian Creek. A young mother tied a rope around her neck and jumped into the water. A passerby spotted her. A big rock held her head down; only her feet were sticking out of the water. People said she took her own life because she had the baby blues.

Grandma brought Annie some tea. It was made of roots that she dug and boiled. She knew a lot of Indian remedies. Every time she drank, they gave her the tea instead of water. Annie snapped out of the depression in a few weeks. They did not know if the tea was the only reason for her recovery. Grandma had a lot of faith in her remedies.

Somebody had to stay with Annie, while Jessie worked. They had to take care of Rachel, the couple's three year old. One day Rachel fell off the porch. When Annie heard her scream, she jumped out of bed and ran to her.

She got there before, whoever was watching the child, could pick her up. Annie didn't go back to bed. She stayed up to take care of her child. After a long struggle, she finally became the wife and mother she had once been.

"The Horse thief"

I am leaving Short in the 1930's and going back to the year 1860. The civil war started. Many women and children were left to take care of their homes and work the farms, while the men were away fighting in the war. Lycurges joined the Confederacy. He was the older brother that Indiana had lived with since she was a baby. He was in the Alabama 11th Calvary.

Indiana's grandchildren tell a story that happened during the year of 1862, That was the year soldiers were fighting in this area. Indiana was 18 years old. She was plowing her crops, with a horse and a single-tree plow. A soldier rode up. He unhooked her horse from the plow, and rode away on it. The horse he left was starved, and rode to death. Indiana turned it loose in her pasture. She expected to find it dead the next morning. She doctored and fed it, and the horse did survive. She felt lucky that she survived. Knowing how desperate the soldiers were, scared her. Fighting was going on at Eastport, Corinth, and at Iuka that year.

Indiana Bugg married Robert Taylor Brown in 1873. Robert was born in Lauderdale Co. Ala. in the Panther Creek area. His home was just up the Tennessee River from Short, Miss. Back then the river was a smaller channel of water, that people crossed frequently. The Tennessee and Alabama side of the river was more populated because it had been settled 16 years earlier. People visited friends and family, and went to church meetings across the river. They stayed in close contact.

Robert Taylor Brown was the son of Thomas Hutchison Brown and Emily Caroline Palmore. Thomas Brown, Robert's father rode a wagon train from North Carolina to Waynesboro, Tennessee. About thirty families traveled together. They settled in Lauderdale County north of Waterloo around 1840. They were part of a great migration of wagon trains bringing settlers to this area. Land could be bought for one dollar an acre.

In 1880, Indiana and Robert Brown made their home on the Mississippi side of the river in Tishomingo County. Probably in the old Bugg home place. Since they lived in the house with Amelia, Indiana's mother. Amelia lived with them until she died the same year, at the age of 76. Indiana Bugg and Robert Taylor Brown had three children:

Mary Eveline Brown, who married Tom Grisham.
William Taylor Brown, who married Sarah Bell Busby
Minnie Tennessee Jane Brown, who married Sam Osborn.

Sam and Minnie Jane Osborn

CHAPTER 4

OSBORN FAMILY -
HUBBARD SALEM

Sam Osborn was born in Marion County Alabama to William Riley Osborn and Susan Holcomb. His family moved to Tishomingo County in 1880. Sam lived in the Hubbard Salem Community when he met Minnie Jane Brown, They were married in 1901.

Indiana and Robert's youngest child Minnie Jane Osborn, died in 1913. The whole Osborn family had typhoid fever. Sam and the children survived. The girls fever went so high their hair came out. They were critical for a long time. Sam Osborn's sister, Aunt Bett moved in with them, and helped take care of the family. Someone had to sit by them day and night. They kept a cool, wet rag on their forehead. They fanned them with a peach tree limb. The keen sound kept the flies away.

Aunt Bett stayed with the family for several years, and helped her brother raise the children. Cora, Sam's daughter, told how Aunt Bett taught them to keep house at an early age. She would stand her in a chair, and let her wash dishes. She taught them how to cook and sew, and take care of themselves.

Annie, the oldest girl, always felt like Paul was her child. He was only eighteen months old when his mother died. Annie became his little mother. She didn't marry until she was thirty-two, because she didn't want to leave her brothers and sister.

Sam and Minnie Jane's home was located at Mark Springs. The spring was named for a Mark family that had lived here before the 1870's. The road to their house was located between Hubbard Salem Church and Hubbard cemetery. There is a big cedar tree where you turned to go down in the hollow to their house. When Ben and Paul Osborn would plow their fields, they always went around this tree. Old graves of the Mark family are located here.

The grandkids tell about picking huckleberries that grew around the spring. Aunt Bett made pies out of their berries. Annie carried on the tradition. Her huckleberry pie is the best pie I've ever eaten. Every time she cooked one she talked about her mother. I know it brought back childhood memories.

Children of Sam Osborn and Minnie Jane Brown were:

Lee Robert Osborn b.1902
Annie Gertrude Osborn b.1904
William Ben Osborn b.1906
Cora Evelyn Osborn b.1909
Robert Paul Osborn b.1912

"Chicken and Dumplings"

Annie Osborn's grandchildren remember a story about how she killed her first chicken. Most of the family would pick up a chicken and wring its head off. After flopping around in the yard, it would bleed out. They would dip it in hot water and pluck the feathers. Cut it up. It was ready to cook.

Annie could not make herself grab one. She was terrified of being flogged or pecked. Well, the day came when it was her time to cook chicken and dumplings. She had cooked it before, but the chicken was always provided. Today, everyone was at work.

Corn, was sprinkled under a metal tub, that was propped up with a stick. When a chicken stuck its head under the tub, Annie sat on it. While that chicken's head was trapped, she cut it off with an axe. For dinner, she had chicken and dumplings, with homemade biscuits and blackberry jam.

Indiana's husband Robert Taylor Brown died in 1916. Indiana moved in the house with her son William Taylor Brown. He was married to Sarah Busby. She lived with Will Brown's family from 1916 to 1932 when she died at age 76. Their home was located at the later home site of Joe Grisham. He was Indiana's great grandson. Joe and Bernice Grisham lived here until they sold the land for the Yellow Creek Nuclear Plant.

Will Brown Sarah Busby Brown

Children of William Taylor Brown and Sarah Busby were:
Eunice Viola Brown- b. 1906
Ruth Gertrude Brown
Herbert O. Brown b.1910
Arther L. Brown b.191
Robert E. Brown b.1918

Eunice Brown married Sidney Johnson. Prentiss, County.
Ruth Brown married Oscar Holland. Prentiss County and Iuka.
They are buried at Hubbard Salem Cemetery.

In the 1880 census, the Bugg families lived on the Hubbard Salem Road in Short. That road started at Hubbard Salem Church, passed Hubbard Cemetery, passed Anna Falls and circled back to the church on Red Sulfur Road. Robert and Indiana Brown, Amelia Bugg lived in house 330. Robert's mother Emily had remarried Doctor Mark Wisdom, They lived next door in house 331. Caroline Hubbard lived in house 336. Lycurges Bugg's house number was 338. Syd Bugg lived at house 326. Louisa Bugg and husband, Bluford Clinton Reynolds, lived in house 315. The houses looked similar, but some were more up to date than others.

Syd Bugg lived in a log house with a dog trot porch. Annie Osborn remembers sitting in straight chairs on his front porch. Everything in his house was made by hand. He loved the old way of living. Feather pillows, corn shuck mattresses, wood heat, and a spring for a refrigerator. Syd loved to make things out of cedar. In his attic was a beautiful, handmade cedar coffin. Just one less thing the family would have to worry about.

Grisham Family - Red Sulfur Road

Mary Evelyn Brown and Thomas Henry Grisham's children were:
William Joseph Grisham b.1894
Miles Herbert Grisham b.1896
Robert Lawrence Grisham b. 1897
Charles Floyd Grisham b.1900
Arthur Clyde Grisham b. 1903
Della Missouri Grisham b.1905
Ernest H. Grisham b. 1907
Dora Belle Grisham b.1913
Una Pearl Grisham b. 1917

Evelyn and Tom Grisham

Evelyn and Tom Grisham were known as Aunt Ed and Uncle Tom to their brother and sister's family. Indiana's two son n laws, Sam Osborn and Tom Grisham were close as brother's. They helped each other work, and when they had to travel, they usually went together.

Descendants told how Papa Sam and Uncle Tom would take their horse and wagon and meet river boats that stopped at Cook's Landing. Especially every fall, after making a crop, supplies to last through the winter would be purchased. They would buy flour in a 100 lb. barrel. Sugar and salt in 50 lb. sacks. They only bought what they could not raise or make. Hogs were raised. They also hunted to furnish meat for the family. Cornmeal could be milled. A lot of fruits and vegetables, were dried or canned to preserve them. Some of Indiana's great grandkids told about picking elderberry buds to place in bags of dried peas. That kept the weevils away.

In the 1900's settlement centered around Hubbard Salem Church. The oldest grave in the Hubbard Salem Cemetery dates to 1876. A few date to the 1880's. Most are buried in the 1900's. Indiana Brown and five generations of her children and grandchildren are buried at Hubbard Salem Church. It was named after the Hubbard family that donated land for the church. That was Caroline Bugg's father n law.

For years, many of the Thomas Jefferson Bugg and Amelia Crawford Bugg family met at the Hubbard Salem Church, once a year on decoration day. The crowd has quit coming, since most of the families have moved away. Indiana's grandchildren were all born at Hubbard Salem. The area is no longer known as Short. Only the water tank bears the name Short. Grandchildren started leaving in the 1940's after the economy of the area fell, and have continued to leave until the 1980's. Some left when the Yellow Creek Nuclear Plant was built.

Billie Bonds told me a memory she had of Hubbard Salem Church. It probably took place in the 1930's. A week long revival was going on at Hubbard Salem. Most of the people came to church in horse pulled wagons or they walked.

Dorman Bugg, Lee bell Davis, Bub Reynolds

Bub Reynold's, Indiana's nephew, bought a T Model car. He brought it to the revival. The building was packed full. Only the women went inside. The church was lit with coal oil lamps. All of the windows were open. The men stood around the building on the outside, or sit on the back of their wagons. They could hear through the windows. Tom Grisham brought a barrel of water and a dipper. Bub was asleep on the steering wheel of his car. Some thought he was probably afraid to leave it. Some of the young men took ropes and tied the car to a tree. When Bub tried to leave, his tires spun. He was stuck!

Bub Reynolds must have been quite a character. Indiana's grandkids didn't know him until he came to visit them. He drove a team of mules and a wagon from Texas. They didn't know how long it took him to get there, but it must have been weeks. He turned his mules loose in pastures along the way. He camped and built fires out of manure piles that he picked up in the pastures. They had to keep a fire going at night to keep the bears away from the livestock.

When he came to Ed and Tom Grisham's, they sit up most of the night. When they slept, they made pallets with quilts. Some slept on the floor in the house, others slept on the porch. Bub slept in his wagon. Later he moved back to Hubbard Salem from Texas. Bub and his wife Lula are buried in the Hubbard Cemetery.

The Grishams always had plenty of food to eat! Sunday evenings were often full of people. Samuel Johnson brought a wagon full of people. Mama Ed killed a couple chicken's and made dressing and dumplings. She also made the best bread. She let yeast set in a snuff glass overnight. The next day when it rose to the top, she made bread. She always had fresh garden vegetables. There was molasses, jams, and jellies.

The kids always let the guest eat first. Sometimes, all they got to eat was molasses and bread, but they never left the table hungry. The children helped make homemade hominy, which was their favorite thing to eat.

"Tom's Smoke House and Corn Crib"

The Grishams kept a smoke house. When they killed hogs, they salted hams to preserve them, and smoked the meat with hickory limbs. Their canned sausage was delicious on cold winter mornings. After hogs were killed, they fried sausage. Several patties were stacked in glass jars, and turned upside down. The grease sealed the top of the jar.

People had to lock their smokehouses and corn cribs. One day, Tom came in and told Mama Ed that one of their ham's was missing. He told her not to tell anyone. Not even the children. Later that month, he picked up a man, and gave him a ride in the wagon. The man asked him if he found the man that stole his ham? Tom said," I have now! Nobody else knew about it". The man jumped off the wagon and ran.

Another time, Tom noticed his crib was missing some corn. He set a large trap by the door. (Probably a bear trap) He caught the thief in the trap. The man had to sit there until he set him free. Of course, he gave an excuse for being there. Tom bandaged his leg, and fed him breakfast. Then he gave him a sack of corn, and told him to never come back to his corn crib. He wouldn't be responsible for what would happen to him, if he did.

Mama Ed kept a barrel at the end of the porch to catch rain water. Joe, their oldest son, often brought a quilt out, and slept on the porch during the hottest time of the year. One night he walked off the porch and fell in the rain barrel. They used that rainwater to wash clothes.

The Grishams also had a well. Sometimes during the hottest part of summer, they would put their milk in the water bucket, and lower it into the water, to keep it cool. Once Ed spilled the milk in the well. The kids had to help draw the well dry, to get the milk out.

They ate milk and bread every week. Sometimes the cows would eat bitter weeds. The milk tasted terrible! The kids had to pull up all the bitter weeds they saw in the pasture.

In the 1930's, an ice peddler came around. They bought a block of ice, wrapped it in quilts, and put it in the fireplace. Mama Ed loved to make iced tea. In the winter, she froze some ice, and made her iced tea. She kept the ice wrapped in a quilt in the storm house to keep it from melting.

In the late 1930's and early 1940's school was held at Hubbard Salem Church. Most of the students were descendants of Amelia and

Thomas Bugg. Rachel Mann said Mrs. Leo Nichols was the teacher. She taught several grades in the same school. It was Easter. She took the whole school to a ridge located behind Hubbard Salem Church. An old log cabin stood on the ridge. It was where church was held before the new Church was built. She spread a quilt on the ground. The children brought their lunch pails and ate under a dogwood tree. Mrs. Nichols picked a blossom off the tree and taught the lesson of the dogwood and Christ's resurrection.

Hubbard Salem School Group About 1940 - Front Row - left to right - Dorman Bullard, Leonard Paul Osborn, Gerald Grisham, James Grisham, Ansel Jones, Faye Davis, Rachel Mann, Carlton Parker, and Woodford Jones Back Row - Leon Davis, James Calvin Lard, James Edward Bullard, Robert Earl Osborn, Billie Ruth Bullard, Houston Bullard, Christine Jones, Hilda Grisham, Dorothy Jones, Lois Jones, and Miss Leo Broughton (teacher)

Annie, who was mom to her younger sister Cora, came to stay a week. During the 1930's, the Bullard family lived on the Red Sulfur road near Short. Cora was in the bed, after one of her children was born. Annie washed the baby and kept a band around its stomach until the cord turned loose of the navel.

She also had a lot of clothes to wash. Water was heated in a kettle on the fireplace. After scrubbing them on a small wooden washboard. Annie hung the wash on the clothes line to dry. All except the step-ins (panties), they hung behind the cook stove until they dried. She was not going to hang them where they could be seen by men and boys.

Cora Osborn and Clement Bullard Family

"Pass the sweet potatoes"

One year, the family gathered at Eunice and Paul Osborn's house for Thanksgiving dinner. They may have had turkey, but Annie brought something special to her younger brother's house. The kids could not wait to take the lid off of a long pot. Their aunt Annie was the best cook. Looking them in the eye was a cooked possum in a bed of sweet potatoes. They knew better than to refuse food. As the platter was passed, each took a little sweet potato and hoped it did not touch that possum. After dinner most of the young people walked to Anna Falls. Paul's daughter, Jennie was a child. She remembers the steep hill they had to go down, to get to the water. To keep from falling, she straddled a tree, until the others came back.

"Lee bell's mule"

Many farmers used mules to pull wagons, farm their crops, and log, until the 1950's. Lee bell Davis had a big white mule named Bell. Mules are known for being stubborn animals. Lee bel was a very big man; He could toss a large stick of stove wood in one hand. During one of these stubborn spells, He hauled of and hit that mule right between the eyes. The grandkids ran to the house. "Grandpa killed our mule! All four feet are sticking up. You said they are reaching for Heaven." Well, the mule was not dead. It was just knocked out. After that, if you saw Lee bell around Hubbard Salem, he was always on his white mule.

Today, only two of Indiana's great grandchildren live in the Hubbard Salem area. Gerald Grisham and Billie Bonds. She married Toy Jr. Bonds. Her parents was Della Grisham and Charley Bullard.

Gerald Grisham parents were Herb Grisham (Herbert Miles) and Doanie Tucker. He married Willie Gaines and later Mildred Barnes.

Billie told me a memory she had of her grandmother, Mary Evelyn Grisham. She was a tiny little woman. She probably didn't weigh 100 pounds. She said her grand daughters would make a saddle by locking their hands and arms together. They would carry Mama Ed across the front porch.

Mama Ed wore her hair in a little ball on top of her head. One day, they told her something they learned in church: A woman's hair is her glory! "Mama Ed, You sure don't have very much glory!"

BackRow: Will Brown. Dorman Bugg
Front Row: Abel Bugg, Tom Grisham

Some of the family moved to Prentiss Co. around the 1940's when sharecropping became profitable on the big farms there. The rich river bottom farmland, that the Bugg family had settled on, was lost when Pickwick Lake was formed in 1939.

Will Brown, Indiana's son, moved his family to Prentiss County. Will and his wife were brought back to Hubbard Salem Cemetery for burial. Most of his children stayed in Prentiss Co.

Two of the Osborn grandchildren also moved to Prentiss Co. Lee and Kate Osborn, and Cora and Clement Bullard raised their families there. Most lived on Gaston Road near Booneville.

Most of the Osborn grandchildren and great grandchildren moved to Iuka, which was only eleven miles away.

Annie Osborn married Jessie Lee Mann. In 1940's they moved to Iuka.

Ben Osborn married Nancy Johnson. Ben's family moved to Iuka after TVA bought their land for the nuclear plant. He also had a son that lived in Huntsville, Ala. Ben and Nancy are buried in Hubbard Salem Cemetery.

Paul Osborn married Eunice Johnson. After Paul died in 1962, Eunice and part of the children, joined the other children that lived in Iuka. They also had a daughter, Jennie that lived in Florence Ala. Paul and Eunice are buried in Hubbard Salem Cemetery.

Several of the Grisham grandchildren made their home in Iuka. They are buried at Hubbard Salem Cemetery.

Joe Grisham, wife Bernice
Herbert Grisham, wife Doanie Tucker
Della Grisham, husband Charley Bullard

Lawrence Grisham, wife Mary Ethel
Floyd Grisham, wife Pauline
Pearl Grisham, husband Kirby Milligan
Ernest Grisham, wife Mattie

Dora Grisham, husband Luther Roberts lived in Counce, Tenn.
Clyde Grisham, wife Ruth Irene lived in Kingston, Tenn.

Lawrence, Floyd, Pearl, and Earnest Grisham are all buried in Oak Grove Cemetery in Iuka, Miss.

Descendants of the Bugg family described the falls before Pickwick Lake was formed. The pool was smaller but much deeper. If you tied a rock to a ball of twine, the twine would run out before you touched bottom. The depth was estimated to be 100 ft. deep from the top. That hole of water joined the river. The old river channel ran close to the bank. Many of the earliest settlers farms were across the river in this area. The deep pool filled with dirt, after timber was cut along Cooper Creek.

Anna Brown died in 1932.

In 1935, a TVA survey of families to be relocated, showed that ten of Indiana's heirs owned 130 acres of her last remaining land. In 1939 TVA bought this land. Part of it formed Pickwick Lake and the perimeter lands around the lake. When filled, the falls no longer emptied into the river, but into Pickwick Lake.

Because of the close location to a state park, most people know this body of water as JP Coleman Waterfalls. From the time Tishomingo County began, until the 1960's, they were known as the "Anna Brown" or "Anna" Falls. Especially to the many descendants of the Bugg family.

Sources:

Singing Hatchet Women - Mississippi Department of Archives - English Dominion
The Clash of Cultures in the Colonial Period - p. 29 - 30

Chickasaw Chiefs- family stories of Levi and George Colbert by Donna R. Causey
1st administration: Tishomingo County Ms Gen Web.

Chickasaw Land Map and Treaties of 1805, 1816, 1818, and 1832.
Historical markers at Eastport - the bridge that was shelled by gunboats

Eastport, Ms. It's Birth and Death by Irene Barnes

Eastport Ms. 1842 -1892 by Jeff Busby- "Vidette" Iuka Ms. Aug. 5, 1946.
Federal Census of 1830 Georgia

Melvin Davis- story of the white mule

Federal Census Miss. District 4, 1840, 1850, 1860.
Ancient Chickasaw Domain Map from Arrell M. Gibson's The Chickasaw 1971.

Federal Census Miss. Tishomingo Co. District 1, 1870, 1880.

1860 Map of old Tishomigo County
Maps, land plats, and family information from Dorvell Bugg

Land descriptions, cemetery plats of Hubbard Salem cemetery and Hubbard Cem. from Dorvell Bugg- great, great grandson of Thomas Jefferson Bugg and Amelia Crawford Bugg.

Pictures from Rachel Welch, Pearl Milligan - granddaughters of Anna Brown

Civil War story, Baby story, Minnie Jane Osborn story, from Annie Osborn Mann Carlisle, granddaughter of Anna Brown.

Location of the old short Post Office from Clyde Grisham as told to Billie Bonds
Ed and Tom Grisham stories from Billie Bonds - great granddaughter of Anna Brown

Stories of Hubbard Cemetery from Genie Johnson - grand daughter of Caroline Bugg and Green Finley Hubbard

Chickasaw dictionary compiled by Jessie Humes and Vinnie Mae Humes 1973.

1935 TVA Survey of families to be relocated by Pickwick Lake.

Stories and pictures of the Hubbard Family from Barbara Sanders - granddaughter of Arizonia Hubbard Sanders, great-great granddaughter of Caroline Bugg and Green Finley Hubbard

History of old Tishomingo County Mississippi - Records from 1836 to 1870 - located in Archives Alcorn County Courthouse Corinth, Mississippi - deeds and land patents.

Johnson Family stories - Marshall Johnson

History of Iuka and Tishomingo County with highlights through 1975: July 1, 1976 Tishomingo County News

I am one of the thousands of descendants of Amelia Crawford and Thomas Jefferson Bugg that live in Alcorn, Prentiss, or Tishomingo County. I belong to the fifth generation of their descendants. Five generations are buried at Hubbard Salem Church. Up to 10 generations have passed since Amelia and Thomas Jefferson Bugg made their home on the land, that would become Tishomingo County Mississippi

Amelia Crawford's genealogy

Amelia's parents were Rachel Sinquefield (1772 - 1823) and Anderson Crawford (1764 -1818). They lived in Columbia County Georgia. The family home was called "Oak Hill". Four generations of Crawfords lived in this house in Appling, Georgia. Anderson served as sheriff of Columbia County.

Anderson's parents were Jane Maxwell (1740-1814) and Charles Crawford (1738-1813)

Charles was the first in this family to move from Virginia to Georgia. He served in the Revolutionary War as a Captain. He, along with three of his son's, received land grants in Georgia for their service.

Before the Revolutionary War began, Charles Crawford served as a delegate in Virginia. He was pressured by the Loyalist to vote against the war. When the vote did not go to their liking. Charles was visited by a group of masked loyalist led by a man named Underwood. They burned his barn and destroyed his home. When they were about to kill his fifteen year old son, Charles pleaded for his son's life. He probably agreed to support their cause. Later Charles was charged with taking a message to South Carolina to a military camp. At night, he loaded his family, and headed to South Carolina. There he joined the Continental Army. Two of his son's also joined with him.

Charles Crawford's parents were Ann Anderson (1708-1802) and David Crawford III (1697-1766). They lived in Amhearst, Virginia. Their family home was called "Tusculum".

David's parents were Elizabeth Smith (1673-1766) and Captain David Crawford II (1662-1762). Born in Jamestown, Virginia Colony, 1662, David Crawford II was the first in this family to be born in America.

David Crawford's II parents were Jane Ann C. Douglas (1633-1710) and Colonel David Crawford Sr. (1625-1710). He, along with his family, were the first Crawford's in this family, to migrate from Northern Ireland to Jamestown, Virginia Colony. David Sr. was born in Kilbirnie, Aryshire, Scotland. He died in 1710, at Assassquin, a large plantation in New Kent Virginia. The entire city of Richmond Virginia, sits on land once owned by Colonel David Crawford. Some think he probably got a land grant from King Charles. The Crawford family supported the king's fight to reign England. He also got large plats of land because he brought groups of twenty settlers to Virginia, and paid their passage on a ship.

Colonel Crawford's parents were Mary Margaret Cunningham (1597-1631) and John, Earl of Crawford (1600-1634). The eldest Crawford heir inherited the entire Crawford estate. Since John didn't inherit anything, he decided to come to Jamestown to seek his fortune. John was killed in the Bacon Rebellion. Jamestown was burned and never rebuilt. The capital of the Virginia Colony was moved to Williamsburg. He was on the side that planned the rebellion against Jamestown and the English governor.

Thomas Jefferson Bugg Genealogy

Thomas Bugg's parents were Lydia Andrews (1769-1833) and Jacob Edmund Bugg II (1749-1825).

Jacob was born in Virginia. He moved to Columbia County, Georgia. Like many other early settlers in Georgia, They came, because of Bounty Land Grants awarded to Revolutionary War Patriots. There he served as a delegate to the Georgia Provincial Congress. Lydia's parents were Mary Buer Philbin and Benjamin Andrews. Benjamin was a Patriot that was a delegate to the 1st Continental Congress. He worked on the Declaration of Independence.

Jacob Bugg's parents were Nannie Obedience Hatcher (1726 - 1786) and Edmund Bugg (1728 - 1786). He lived in Mecklenburg County, Virginia when he died.

Edmund Bugg's parents were Sarah Bacon(1691-1756) and Samuel Bugg III (1691 - 1756). Samuel was born in Virginia Colony, New Kent County. He died in Lunenburg County, Virginia.

Samuel parents were Deborah Sherwood (1669 - 1715) (Sherwood Forest in England) and Samuel Bugg II (1640 - 1716). Samuel was the first member of this family to come to Virginia Colony. He settled in Jamestown. He came from Brandeston, Suffolk, England.

Samuel's parents were Marie Dumas (1604 - 1755) and Samuel Bugg I (1599 - 1654).
They lived in Brandeston, Suffolk, England. In England, they spelled their name Bugge.

Grandmother Brown, the mother of Robert Taylor Brown, was a Palmer. Emily Caroline Palmore was the daughter of Elisha Palmore Palmer and Mary Ann Weatherly.

Elisha Palmer associated with abolitionists. He was active in the underground railroad. After his activities were discovered, he escaped through the same route that he helped many black families use. In his house in Florence, Lauderdale County Alabama, he had a secret room built in the wood shed. It sheltered many on the underground railroad. Here they boarded a boat that followed a route on the Tennessee river, past Paducah, Kentucky into Illinois. It was a free state.

In the book, "Unbroken Chains", a letter is published to William Sill, a leader in the underground railroad. In it descriptions of Florence, Alabama and the steamboat port of Eastport, Mississippi are described. There is no regularity by the steamboats on the Tennessee River. In February of 1851, a passenger paid $1.00 a day for board at a tavern in Eastport. It was one room for all to sleep in. Passengers waited for the steamboat to arrive. Sometimes they were three or four days late. Conditions were described as being wretched. The tavern had a gambling room. There were many taverns in the North, but not many in the South. In Florence, Alabama, many plantation owners opened their homes to travelers.

Elisha died in Kansas. His parents were Martin Palmer and Elizabeth Powers. They lived in Virginia and North Carolina. Martin was the son of Thomas Palmer and Joane Jordan. They were from Yorkshire

England. They arrived in Virginia in 1621. Thomas was the son of Edward Palmer. The Palmer line goes back several generations to Sir Henry De Palmer 1100-1160 in Glorcestershire England.

Grand Children of Minnie Jane Brown and Samuel Thomas Osborn

Children of Kate Bullard and Lee Osborn
1. Robert

Children of Nancy Johnson and Ben Osborn
1. Rafael Osborn
2. Linda Osborn
3. Rayborn Osborn

Children of Annie Osborn and Jessie Lee Mann
1. Rachel Mann (Brumley) (Welch)

Children of Cora Osborn and Clement Bullard
1. Houston Bullard
2. Minnie Jane Bullard (Jumper)
3. Dick Bullard
4. Cliff Bullard
5. Dormon Bullard
6. Shelby Bullard
7. Betty Sue Bullard (Palmer)
8. Glenda Bullard (Harwell)
9. Evelyn Bullard (Davis)

Children of Eunice Johnson and Paul Osborn
1. Leonard Paul (Rast) Osborn
2. Tom Osborn
3. Jennie Osborn (Reynolds) (Moneyham)
4. Raymond Osborn

Brown Genealogy

Minnie Jane Brown (1882-1913) (b. and d. Short, Tishomingo Ms.)
Husband: Sam Osborn (18671937) (b. Marion, Ala.)

Robert Taylor Brown (1848-1916) (b. Lauderdale, Ala. d. Short, Tishomingo, Ms)
wife: Indiana Bugg (1843-1932) (b. and d. Short, Tishomingo Co. Ms.)

Thomas Hutchison Brown (1814-1860) (b. North Carolina d. Lauderdale Ala.)
wife: Emily Caroline Palmore (1826-1900) (b. Tenn. d. Tishomingo, Miss.)

CHAPTER 5

COMPTON - THE RAILROAD BRINGS FAMILY TO BURNSVILLE

Elizabeth Jane Compton moved to Tishomingo County sometime between 1916 and 1920. Jack Compton, passed away while living in Decatur, Alabama in 1916. He left Elizabeth with eight children to raise.

Virgie 1891-1928
Stonewall 1897 -1983
Ruby 1903-1992
Ethel 1903-1989
Rushelia 1905-1987
Ellis 1909-1953
Zettie 1911-
Edward 1912-1989

Elizabeth Ellis Compton

I've heard Edward say he was the 24th child. Elizabeth was Jack's second wife. He had children that lived in Lawrence County Alabama. That is where he lived with his first wife, until after her death.

Before he died, Jack's physical health, as well as his mental health failed. Jack was a horse trader. He lost their farm in a bad trade. Edward said the family was starving to death. Two of the boys from Jack's first family, and Elizabeth's brother, Marion Ellis, worked for the railroad.

At the time, they were laying tracks in Burnsville. Uncle William Ellis moved Elizabeth and the children to Burnsville where he could care for them. Richard and Riley Compton, the older brothers, also took care of the family. Their home was on a hill near the Burnsville water tank. The children grew up. Some went back to Decatur. Others made Burnsville their home

Stonewall became a well-known character in Tishomingo County. He worked at sawmills and farming. Being the older brother, Stonewall took care of the family. They grew up during the depression years. He kept them fed, but he only spent money on necessary things.

Later in life, many considered him a miser. He would not spend a penny unless it came back to him two fold. Stonewall was a good business man. He bought and sold a lot of real estate. He always bought it at a good price because back then, cash talked.

Stonewall could be seen picking up cotton on the side of the roads. Almost every family farm raised cotton. It blowed out of trucks that were headed to the gin in Burnsville. Every September the sides of the road were white during harvest season. Stonewall carried a tow sack with a strap over his shoulder. He walked to town every day picking up cotton as he went. He added these sacks to the cotton he raised, to make a good bale.

His clothes came from the army surplus store. Stonewall always took a bath once a year, whether he needed it or not. He wore his hair long, with a beard. He usually kept a dip of snuff and brushed his teeth with a twig.

Stonewall walked everywhere he went. He never started to Iuka or Corinth unless someone stopped and gave him a ride. On his walks around town, he always found a place to eat a meal. Even though he wouldn't spend money on himself, he always helped any of his friends that were down and out.

Edward Compton told many stories about his older brother.

"The Baptism"

Stonewall could not talk plain. After being around him, his family and friends understood most of what he said. Even though every syllable he spoke came out wrong. When he was a young man he was baptized.

It was a Sunday afternoon. The Burnsville congregation meet at Smith's pond to baptize all of the repenters that had come forward during that week's gospel revival. Six souls were lined up to follow the plan of salvation. Stonewall was first in line.

The preacher waded out in the water up to his waist. Stonewall did not like the idea of being pushed under the water. The preacher said baptism was a part of salvation. Too save his soul, he was going to do this.

The congregation sang," Shall we gather at the river. "Stonewall waded into the water. The preacher asked if he believed that Jesus Christ was the son of God. Stonewall answered" yes." The preacher raised his hand and said, "I baptize you in the name of the father, the son, and the Holy Ghost. Just as the preacher put his hand on the neck, ready to lay him back in the water. Stonewall jumped up and said "Nake". The preacher said, "Yes Son, You will be saved". He tried to lay him down again. Wailing his arms, Profanity rang out loud and clear. "G—D— Snake! Snake!" In a split second, Stonewall was out of the water.

We learned something about Stonewall that day. He was afraid of water, but he was even more afraid of snakes. We had never heard him upper a clear syllable until today. Apparently when he gets scared or curses, he can talk plain.

Stonewall was baptized, but not on this Sunday afternoon. They took him to the creek, since he refused to step foot in that pond.

Stonewall's mother was the only person that called her son by his first name. It was a name from her side of the family. If you wanted to make him mad, all you had to do was call him "Bethel". His younger brothers tried that once. He drug them out of the house by the ear and put them to work in the fields. He was "Stonewall" from then on.

"A Mail Order Bride"

One day Stonewall came to his brother's house. Edward often made phone calls for him. He had to be an interpreter since no one could understand a word his brother said. The address above the number read "Mail Order Bride". Edward said, "I hope you are not getting involved in this scam." With perfect speech, Stonewall replied, "You need to mind your own G—D— business" and stomped out of the house.

Edward's sister said Stonewall paid two thousand dollars to have an oriental woman flown to this country. He paid his nephew, Jack to drive to Birmingham to pick her up.

Stonewall paid his lawyer to negotiate for him. After telling him his plans, the lawyer did not want to make the call. "OK, I will get a lawyer that wants my business." The lawyer warned him about legal aspects of marrying anyone. He wrote a contract for her to sign to save his assets. Stonewall said "I am an old man, I am going to have a wife, even if I have to buy her."

Stonewall lived alone in a little shotgun house with two rooms. He did not have an indoor bathroom or water. He had wood heat, but he did not use it unless it was very cold. Stonewall had more money than most of the people in our county, but you could not tell that by the way he lived.

He knew his accommodations were poor. That's the reason he ordered a woman from a foreign country. He did not think she was used to anything better. He also thought it wouldn't matter if he could not speak plain. She probably could not understand the language any way.

Jack picked the bride up at the airport. She seemed to be a pleasant, nice looking, middle aged woman. She wore neat, modern clothes and she spoke enough English to carry on a conversation. The woman was very impressed with the young man that loaded her luggage and drove her to Burnsville. This must be a good family that I go to. They teach their young people to have manners.

It was almost dark when the car drove into the driveway, Stonewall had washed his face and slicked his hair back. He even wore a clean shirt.

When Jack unloaded her luggage, the woman's eyes pleaded, "Don't leave me with him". She slipped out that night, never to be seen again. I don't know how she got away. There was no other transportation there. Stonewall did not own a car. No one in the neighborhood saw her except Jack. Stonewall warned Him, "Never mention this again. Not one word, if you expect to get any of my money."

That call he wanted to make was to get his money back. That did not happen!

Compton Genealogy

Harvey Compton (1947-1994) (b. and d. Burnsville, Tishomingo Co. Ms.)
wife: Betty Brumley (1950) (b. Iuka, Tishomingo Co. Ms.)

Earnest Edward Compton (1912-1989) (b. Trinity, Morgan Co. Ala. d. Burnsville, Ms.)
wife: Esther Seaton (1915-2001) (b. Coles Mill, Tishomingo Co. Ms. d. Burnsville, Tishomingo Co. Ms.)

William Clark Compton (1851-1916) (b. Dallas, Paulding Co. Georgia d. Decatur, Morgan Co. Ala.) The family left Georgia during the civil war, They were in the path of General Sherman, the Union General who left a path of destruction across Georgia in the campaign to burn Atlanta.

wife: Elizabeth Ellis (1874-1953) (b. Pen Hook, Lawrence Co. Ala. d. Decatur, Ala.)

Richard Compton (1813-1911) (b. and d. Clark, Dodge Co. Ga.)
wife: Elizabeth Smith (1811-1880) (b. Edgefield, SC. d. Ellaville, Winston Co. Ala.)

Jehu Compton II (1767-1822) (b. Halifax Co. Va. d. Clarke, Ga. Clark, Ga.)
wife: Martha Frances (Fanny) Scates (1775-1890)

Jehu Compton Sr. (1744-1786) (b. Halifax, Va. d. Warwick, Halifax, Va.)
wife: Mary Smith (1748-1807) (b. and d. Halifax, Va.) Quakers

John Compton (1710-1780) (b. Nottingham, Chester, Penn. d. Halifax, Va.)
wife: Elizabeth Piggott (1720-1747) (b. Chester, Penn. d. Nottingham, Cecil, Maryland)

John Bartholomew Compton (1690-1739)

"The Quakers"

The Religious Society of Friends referred to as the Quakers Movement, was founded in England in the 17th century. The early Friends were persecuted for their beliefs. Quakers rejected elaborate religious ceremonies. Their meetings were silent and reverent. They did not have one speaker. They believed in spiritual equality for men and women. Women were free to speak in their meetings.

Quaker missionaries first arrived in Maryland and Virginia in the 1650's. Many were persecuted in America. The Puritans of Massachusetts executed many between 1650-1660. Quakers regarded all humans as having a soul, that included the Indians and Blacks. They would not take up arms against their fellow man. These beliefs were not tolerated by many colonists.

In 1681 King Charles gave a large land grant to a rich Quaker named William Penn. He founded Pennsylvania as a sanctuary for religious freedom and tolerance. In just a few years several thousand Quakers moved from England to Pennsylvania.

The Compton's were from England. Henry Compton was the Lord Bishop of London. Four generations of this family were Quakers. They are recorded in meetings from Maryland, Pennsylvania, and Virginia. John Bartholomew was first to be recorded in Quaker meetings in West Nottingham, Chester County, Maryland.

The Compton's lived at the edge of William Penn's land grant, this land was on the border of Pennsylvania and Maryland. There was an eighty year land dispute between the two colonies. Both sides claimed the land.

The dispute between the Penn family of Pennsylvania and the Calvert family of Maryland erupted into war in 1730. After much bloodshed and conflict, a ceasefire was negotiated by King George II of England in 1738.

The Penn and Calvert families hired two Englishmen, Mason and Dixon, to mark this official property line. The project took five years to complete. In 1767 it became the border that separated Maryland and Pennsylvania known as the Mason Dixon Line.

It would become the border that divided the slave and non-slave states in the civil war. Many of the Quakers that lived here were abolitionist. They helped many slaves cross the border to freedom.

The Quakers did not socialize or marry outside of their group. They were small farmers and craftsmen that lived a very modest lifestyle. Since they felt responsible for each other's soul and well being. Discipline was used to maintain a high moral character.

Records were kept of each Friend's meeting. Marriages were approved by the Friends. In the Monthly Meeting of Fairfax Friends, 26 day, 7th month - 1747, John Compton and wife Elizabeth Piggott, of Susquehannah Hundred, Cecil Co. Md. asked permission to marry. A group of friends were appointed to question the community about his conduct and character before approval was granted.

In meeting thirteen, they were given a certificate of approval for John Compton and wife to leave Fairfax for another Meeting location.

Jehu Compton II was the last member of this family to be recorded in a Friend's Meeting. He moved from Halifax, Virginia to Clark County, Georgia before 1802.

Source

Encyclopedia of American Quaker Genealogy. Vol. VI Virginia - Fairfax Monthly Meeting
page 484

Interviews: Earnest Edward Compton, Esther Seaton Compton
Interview: Jane Upchurch Chance daughter of Ethel Compton

US, Quaker Meeting Records 1681-1935 Loudoun, Virginia Fairfax Monthly Meeting Minutes 1746-1776 (12)

US Census tishomingo County

Nottingham, Cecil County Maryland Quaker records Book F 1808-1836

US Quaker Meeting Records, 1681-1935 page 396 ; page 37
Quaker editor, History

The Seaton family - Coles Mill

William Thomas Seaton was born February 22, 1883 in Hardin County, Tennessee. He was the youngest child of William M. Seaton and Betty Elizabeth Austin. Most of his young life was spent in the Holland Creek area of Hardin County Tennessee. Will had four siblings:

James D. Seaton (1867-1897)
Matilda Seaton (1871-1896)
Mary Etta Seaton (1874 - 1896)
Harriet R. Seaton (1878)

James Seaton married Josie Blackburn on November 6,1892 in Hardin County, Tennessee. Enoch Austin signed a bond for $1,200.00 so that they could get married. Enoch was James mother's uncle. This type of bond for couples to wed was customary at the time. The signer had to be able to put up that amount of property or money before they signed the bond.

James and Josie had one child, Clara Ethel Seaton, born Jan.23,1894. Clara married Creed Kimberling and moved to Fort Worth, Texas. She kept in touch with her Uncle Will Seaton until his death. I have several Christmas cards that she sent him. I don't know the exact date of James death. Josie married again in 1898.

Richard Woodruff remembered a story Papa Seaton told when he was a boy. Will and James were hoboing to Florida to find work. When they got to Iuka, Will wanted to stay. His future wife, Maxie had moved here. His brother wanted to go on to Florida. Will waved at his brother when the train pulled out. That was the last time Will saw James. He never heard from him again.

Matilda Seaton married Henry Glidewell Jan.4, 1890. They had three children:

John Clarence Glidewell
Rena P. Glidewell
Grady Glidewell

Will Seaton was an orphan. He lost his mother in 1891, when he was eight years old. His father and 2 sisters died in 1896, the year he turned 13. His father died from consumption (tuberculosis). The 1880 census placed Will as living just a few houses away. He lived with his Grandmother, Mary Poppy Qualls Seaton, after his mother died. He also had Qualls and Austin cousins that lived in the Holland Creek area. Will may have lived with them.

The 1900 census of McNairy County, Tennessee showed Will Seaton living in Stantonville, Tennessee when he was 17 years old. A boarder in the home of Henry Glidewell. Henry was a sawmill operator. Henry's first wife was Matilda Seaton, Will's sister. She died 4 years earlier and Henry had married again.

Will worked at the sawmill as a teamster. He drove a wagon pulled by a team of mules, that hauled the logs and lumber. Will remained a teamster until he died. He kept mules and a wagon even after he bought his first car in the 1940's.

Maxie Seaton told her grandchildren she met Will on a farm in Stantonville. They were both orphans that worked on the same farm during harvest time.

Maxie Viola Fields and William Thomas Seaton married March 2, 1902 at the Alcorn County Courthouse in Corinth, Ms. He was nineteen and she was fourteen.

Maxie lived in Kendrick, Ms. at that time, with her father, Jack Fields and his second wife, Amanda Greenhall. Her mother, Malissa Corhom Fields died in 1895, when she was only eight years old. Maxie and her brother Dick Fields were born in Olive Hill, a small town in Hardin County Tennessee.

Will and Maxie moved down Kendrick road a few miles. They bought a farm in Coles Mill. The couple raised their family there. They lived on the same farm for almost sixty years.

"The Happy Hollow Ghost"

Some of the Seaton children went to school at Mulberry which was located in a nearby church. It was a mile away. A group of neighbor's kids walked to school together. Later they went to Barnes Chapel. The school was only a half-mile from the Seaton farm. Since it was so close, they often walked home alone.

The kids had to cross a branch on Happy Hollow road. They heard strange moaning sounds. OOOOOOOOOOOOO! OOOOOOOOOO! All the kids ran through the water and headed home, as fast as they could go. Will wanted to know why they were so wet and scared. It had to be a ghost they said. No animal that we know, makes a sound like that. It was so scary.

The next morning, Will made a trip to the local whiskey still. It was probably kin folks that made whiskey. "Quit scaring my kids." "I'll see to it that they want bother you". "I don't want to see them frightened again."

At the supper table that night, Will had an eerie sound in his voice as he spoke words of warning. "There are some bad, bad spirits haunting that hollow! They have been there for a long, long time. Never, ever, leave the road and always stick together. If you don't bother them, they want bother you."

We never forgot those ghosts. You didn't have to warn a Seaton child to stay off of Happy Hollow Road at night.

Will was a Do-it-Yourself kind of guy. He even did most of his own doctoring. Esther recalls a day when he cut his arm on a piece of tin. He took a crooked needle out of a box. After cleaning it with peroxide, he sewed up his own cut.

Will and Maxie had 12 children. 4 of their young children are buried at Mulberry Cemetery.

Infant son (1907)
Infant son (1908)
Willie Seaton (1910 -1911)
Berthie Seaton 1917 - 1921) (cause of death- Diptheria)

Mary Seaton (1905-1980) married Andrew Morris
Myrtle Seaton (1909-1973) married Johnny Woodruff
Ruby Seaton (1912 - 1937) married Alfred Whitaker
Homer Seaton (1918 - 1981) married Inez White
Vedie Seaton (1922 - 1967) married Addison Reynolds
John Dee Seaton (1924 -1988) married Dois Lambert
Rhoda Seaton (1927 - 2008) married Charles Green

Will Seaton followed his future wife, Maxie Fields, to Tishomingo County in 1902. Four generations of Will's family, (Seaton, Qualls, Austin, Lambs) lived in Hardin County in Lowryville, Hubbardsville, and Holland Creek areas. This area is located between Waterloo, Ala. and Savannah, Tn.

Many wagon trains brought families to Wayne County Tennessee. They settled the areas around Second Creek in Wayne County, Bumpass Creek in Lauderdale County, and Holland Creek in Hardin County. This migration started in 1820 when the land opened for settlement. It lasted for thirty years.

Will's grandpa, Captain Baldy (Stephen) Austin led over 30 trains from North Carolina to Wayne County, Tn.

Around 1957, Will and Maxie sold their farm at Coles Mill (Doskie) and moved to Burnsville. They bought an antebellum house that was used as a union hospital during the civil war. On April 17, 1962, Will died at the age of 79. He is buried at Pleasant Grove Church of Christ near his old home place. Maxie lived on in Burnsville until she died in 1977 at the age of 90.

Will and Maxie Seaton

Will and Maxie Seaton had 24 grandchildren.

Lorene Morris married Carl Lynch

Alton Morris
Hershel Morris
Neladene Morris
Roy Morris
Billy Morris
Faye Morris
Jimmy Morris
Sue Morris
Bobby Morris

Donna Morris
Howard Woodruff married Lottie Brown
Geneva Woodruff married Robert Osborn
Richard Woodruff married Ruth Durham
Juanita Woodruff married Clifford Carlisle
Ray Gene Woodruff married Libby Maxwell
WT Whitaker
Vedena Whitaker
Harvey Compton married Betty Brumley
Vernita Seaton married David Sitton
Joan Seaton married Danny Lynch
Ronald Seaton married Debbie Dill; Diane Tumlinson
Wayne Green

The Seaton Family- Will, Maxie, Esther. Myrtle, Ruby, Mary,

Will, Maxie, and Myrtle Seaton at a store in Doskie

Seaton Genealogy

William Thomas Seaton (1883-1962) (b. Holland Creek, Hardin Co. d. Burnsville, Ms.)
wife: Maxie Viola Fields (1887-1977) (b. Olive Hill, Hardin Tn. d. Burnsville, Tishomingo Ms.)

William M. Seaton (1846-1896) (b. and d. Hardin Tn.)
wife: Betty Elizabeth Austin (1847-1891) (b. and d. 8th district Hardin Tn.)

James H. Seaton(1827-1912) (b. Holland Creek, HardinTn.)
wife: Mary Poppy Qualls (1828-1880) (b. Wayne Tn. d. Holland Creek, Hardin Tn.)

Soloman Seaton (1804-1880) (b. Va. d. Hardin Tn.)
wife: Maria Berry (1802-1871) (b. Ga. d. HardinTn.)

Moses Seaton (1767-1859) (b. Stafford, Va. d. Henderson, Tn.)
wife: Rosanna Martin (1769-1869 Married Sevier, Tn.) (b. N.C. d. Henderson, Tn.)

James Seaton (1720-1823)

The name" Seaton" Scottish; means "Sea Town"

Fields Genealogy

Maxie Viola Fields (1887-1977) (b. Olive Hill, Hardin Co. Tn. d. Tishomingo Co. Ms.)
husband: William Thomas Seaton (1883-1962)

Jack Fields (1862-1905) (b. Lauderdale, Tn. d. Alcorn, Ms.)
wife: Malissa Corhom (1860-1895)

John Everett Fields (1831-1906) (b. Williamson, Tn. d. Lauderdale, Tn.)
wife: Mary Elizabeth Turner (1838-1910) (b. Williamson, Tn. d. Lauderdale, Tn.)

Samuel Jackson Fields (1802-1850) (b. N.C. d. Lauderdale, Tn.)
wife: Jemima Barnes (1803-1848) (b. Rockingham, N.C. d. Lauderdale, Tn.)

Allen Fields (1770-1850) (b. Rowan, NC- d. Williamson, TN.)

Nathaniel Fields Jr. (1725-1777) (b. Hanover, Va. d. Guilford, NC)
Revolutionary War Soldier
wife: Mary Dodd Armstrong (1725-1797) (b. Rockingham, NC d. Rockingham, NC)

Nathaniel Fields Sr. (1709-1763) (b. Va. d. NC)
wife: Sarah Ann Lawson (1710-1790) (b. and d. Lancaster, Va.)

William John Fields (1698-1748)(b. and d. Lancaster Pa.)
wife: Elizabeth Jane Powell (1700-1772) (b. York, Pa. d. Guilford, NC)
John Fields (1664-1740) (b. and d. Tyrone, Lancaster, Pa.)
Mary Elizabeth Ames (Bridgewater, Plymouth, Ma. d. Somerville, Middlesex, Ma.)

Abraham Fields (1636-1674) (b. and d. Va.)
wife: Alice Ellis (1636-1668) (b. and d. Westmoreland, Va.)

Henry Fields (1611-1667) (b. Lincolnshire, Eng. d. Jamestown, Va.)

Sources:

1900 US Federal Census McNairy Co. Tn.
1910 US Federal CensusTishomingo Co.
1920 Us Federal Census Coles Mill, Tishomingo Co. Ms.
1930 US Federal Census Tishomingo Co. Ms.
1940 US Federal Census Tishomingo Co. Ms.
Story of James Seaton; Richard Woodruff
Stories of the Seaton Family; Dois Seaton
Stories of Will Seaton's early years; Rhoda Green
Stories of Holland Creek; Linda Qualls
1850-1880 US Census, Hardin County

In 1933, Esther was born in a log cabin on a hill near Pleasant Grove Church of Christ. She was the daughter of Will and Maxie Seaton of Coles Mill (Doskie), Ms.

Esther and her brothers and sisters walked to school at Mulberry and Barnes Chapel. In a small pail, they carried their lunch. It was usually meat and biscuit. Sometimes they had dried fruit pies, boiled eggs, or sweet potatoes.

Esther's best friend was Ruth Cole. At recess they liked to play pretend games. The girls land had been enlarged by cutting a few trees. Girls played on one side of the school. Boys played on the other side. They also went to the bathroom on their own side. Esther stood on one of those tree stumps and predicted her own future. "When I grow up, I am going to be the wife of a handsome preacher. I'll eat chicken, and I won't have to cook it. "When I grow up I am going to have three girls and three boys. Their names will be: Rose, Lily, and Pink; Fart, Fizzle, and Stink."

Another time, she fell in the creek on her way to school. Being a tomboy, she showed the other girls how to swing from a limb. Esther wore the teacher's coat while her clothes dried. The tree outside the school window was full of petticoats and pantaloons. It looked like someone had hung up a wash. A school bus drove Esther to Burnsville High School. She finished her school years in the 8th grade. That's where she met Edward Compton.

To see Esther, Edward walked a single lane road that wound through forest and swamp from Burnsville to Coles Mill. Most nights there were plenty of others walking along the road. That's how most people got around. They walked or rode on a horse pulled wagon.

One Saturday night, Edward missed his walking pals. He kept staying at the Seatons. He sure was dreading walking alone, through that long, dark bottom, this late at night

Mr. Will brought him a quilt and pillow. He said, "Ed, if you are going to stay all night, you can sleep on the porch." "Everybody to bed, We have church tomorrow." The Seaton family did not miss church. Will Seaton was an elder at the Pleasant Grove Church of Christ.

The only time a boy got to see Esther, was when he walked her home from church. That walking took place with other couples, just behind the family.

Ed really liked to come to revivals. The church had dinner on the ground. It was the best food he had ever tasted. Mr Seaton usually killed a goat, and made hash. Tables were full of cakes, pies, and all kinds of meat. His favorite was chicken and dressing. The church was full for each sermon. People listened through raised windows to the sermon and the most heartfelt singing. The church yard was also full. Most of the men stayed outside. The women usually filled the church. Ed never went to a revival service that did not have a response to the invitation song. Front pews were full of responders each night. The next Sunday, after the revival, they had a big baptizing at yellow creek.

In 1936, Edward and Esther got married at the court house in Iuka, Ms. For a short time, they lived with Edward's mother in Burnsville. A year later, they rented a house on Eastport Street in Burnsville.

Edward went to work on a state highway project. Originally hwy 72 was routed down 45 from Corinth, Selmer, and on to Memphis. In 1935 Hwy 72 was routed through Corinth to Memphis.

Now that Edward had a job, other than farming, they started building their first house. It was a slow go. They would buy a few pieces of lumber or a few nails when they had the money. Esther's dad was a good carpenter. He helped them build with whatever materials they had. After years, they finished half of the house. It had two front doors and two back doors. They could not afford to live in the finished side. Iness and Clay Timbes, their best friends rented the finished side. With the rent money, they slowly finished the entire house. They just finished the entire house when World War II started.

Edward and Esther Compton

"World War II"

Edward joined the Navy in 1943. Two of Esther's brothers, Homer and John Dee Seaton joined the same year. At the beginning of the war, their wives, Dois and Inez Seaton came to Esther's house. During the day, they had all the farm work to do. At night they quilted.

Maxie Seaton, Esther's mom had ordered patterns for all the state birds from Sears and Roebuck. Her chest was full of hand made quilts. She wanted all of her children to have cover for their beds.

That quilt was never finished. They never had time to do another one. All of the women went to work, and they never quit working outside the home.

Esther went to Decatur, Alabama and got a job. She loaded boxcars with gun shells and war supplies. They were transported by rail and by boat, on the Tennessee river.

This was the days of "Rosie the Riveter". The women did their part for the war effort. This country needed women in the work force. Esther stayed with Edward's sisters, who were also there to find jobs. Edward enlisted August 20, 1943. He went through training on the Great Lakes and on to San Francisco.

Esther rode a train from Burnsville to San Francisco. The trip took eight days. Her ankles were swollen as big as her leg. This Mississippi girl had never been more fifty miles from home.

She stayed with her sailor a few weeks, until he shipped out in December. The hotels all along the water front were full of wives, that had come to say "Good Bye". They had no idea when the would see their husbands again.

Edward joined the Pacific fleet December 15, 1943 on the San Jacinto, an aircraft carrier. His ship saw action in the Marianas, Guam, Philippines, and attacks on Japan. One of the most famous pilots on the San Jacinto was George H W Bush.

These aircraft carriers were part of the Trinity Campaign. Over 300 ships were positioned in the Pacific Ocean near Okinawa, Japan. They provided a base for planes to bomb Japan and return to the ship. The main target was Tokyo.

Suicide pilots flew into the ships to do as much damage as possible. The planes carried bombs. When they hit it made a big explosion. Edward was far enough away from an explosion that he was just knocked down. He tried to drag one of his burned comrades out of the flames. The San Jacinto did not take a direct hit.

Nearby ships were not as lucky. Edward asked the Radio officer to check on John Dee Seaton. On April 7, 1945 his ship, the USS

Hancock, took a direct hit from a kamikaze plane. There were many injuries and casualties.

Edward and Esther's only child was Harvey Compton (1947- 1994). A baby boomer that was born when the soldiers returned from the war.

"The Cow Boy"

As a boy, Harvey had several lessons "on making a living". His parents started a bank account for their son, the day he was born. They did not give him a lot of money, but they helped him do projects to earn money. One of those projects was cattle.

When Harvey accumulated enough to buy a cow, he started a herd. His neighbor, Mr. Hall, took him to the cattle auction. Harvey did the bidding. He bought two head for the price of one. This cow was with calf. Mr. Hall carried it back to their pasture in a cattle trailer. He was the only person Harvey knew that owned a trailer. Most of the farmers just had side frames on their pickups. To have a calf, Harvey had to move his cow to a neighbor's pasture. It was not an easy task to get the cow to the bull, which was nearly a mile away. Mr Hall loaned him a rope halter that tied around the cow's nose and head. The plan was to lead it down the road.

He almost got there, when the noose slipped. Fearing the cow would run away, he did not chase it. A few friends, drove it down the road and into the pasture. As he closed the gate, this cowboy knew what his next purchase was going to be.

Mr Hall advised him to get the best bull he could afford. It would upgrade his herd. He drove to a ranch in Amory that raised pure bred cattle. It cost one thousand dollars to buy a Black Angus Bull with papers.

His Daddy said, "That's a lot of money to put in an animal that could lay down and die tonight." Standing in the pasture, it looked like the cover of a farm magazine. I think Mr. Hall thought that was more bull than he needed. For years it sired many calves.

Harvey did not lose that purchase, but he lost other cows and calves. Frank Rhodes was a self-taught farm animal doctor. He made many house calls to the Compton farm.

The herd had grown into thirty-two head. Harvey had to rent another farm to have enough grazing pasture.

One of his cows lay down and could not get up. Harvey fed and watered her where she lay. She was heavy with a calf. In a few days, Frank saved the calf, but the cow was paralyzed.

They tried turning her. They even built a frame and tried to hoist her to her feet. Nothing worked. The cow had to be shot, her calf was raised on a bottle.

Losing one cow was bad enough, but another fell the same way. Frank delivered the calf, but the second cow had to be shot.

We have to figure out what's happening to these animals. If we don't, you are going to lose some more.

The farm had a large lower pasture. It was fairly level with good access to water. Every day, the cattle walked up a hill, through a gap, and on to the barn. Frank picked up a rake. He walked to the gap, and stuck the handle into the mud. It sank two feet. Walking through that mud is what's killing you cows. They took the fence down.

It was an expensive lesson. Thanks to Frank Rhodes, Harvey did not lose any more cows to that mud hole.

"Honky Tonk City"

In the 50's and the 60's there was a migration of southerners to the north. The automobile industry was booming in Detroit, Michigan. Many moved to Chicago, Ill. and Hammond, Indiana for jobs. Edward left tishomingo county with Thomas Burns. They were two of many that joined the carpenter's local and went to work building steel mills in Hammond, Indiana.

For years, Edward only saw his family on holidays. Even though he was away most of his son's life, he never failed to mail his check home. A few times Edward tried to get Esther to move up north with him. He missed them so much!

Esther said, "OK, I'll pack our bags." He said, "No, That Honky Tonk city is no place to raise a child. I'll just work a little longer and retire soon.

He could not find work in the south that would allow him to support his family. In 1966, Edward was making $10.58 cents an hour. His son, Harvey, worked at a local piano factory at the same time. He was making $1.58 cents an hour. Edward retired and came home in 1969. He died in Burnsville in1990.

This Grandpa's number one pleasure, was watching his grand daughters grow up. He raised goats, chickens, pigs just for the girls.

Esther ran an upholstery shop in Burnsville for over 30 years. After Harvey started to school, she went to the unemployment office and applied for work. She did not have any luck getting a job. She was older than most of the factory workers. She went to a trade school, There she learned upholstery skills. With the ability to work hard and a people - pleasing personality, she built a very successful business. Esther lived in Burnsville near her grand daughters until she died in 2001.

Sources:

Fold 3 for military battles and facts about the USS San Jacinto and USS Hancock.

Esther Compton was my biggest source of information about the Compton's and Seaton's. She told the stories of her life as a child growing up at Cole's Mill, her early married days, and what was happening at home during World War II.

Edward and Esther Compton with Grand Daughters,
Cortney and Casey Compton

CHAPTER 6

THE BRUMLEY FAMILY
- SARDIS ROAD

William Brumley and his wife Bessie come to Tishomingo county before1914. Will was born in Franklin County, Alabama March 25, 1872. He was the child of William Thomas Brumley and Martha Clement. He moved from Franklin County Alabama to Hardin County, Tennessee in 1900. On May 7, 1902 he married Bessie Handley at Olive Hill, Tennessee.

Their children were:
Zella Inez Brumley (1904 - 1993) spouse- Ward Parsons
Oris Denver Brumley (1906 - 1982) spouse - Josephine P
Cora Mae Brumley (1909 - 1974) spouse - Oscar Parsons
Herbert Clifford Brumley (1911 - 1980) spouse - Roxie Wilson
Kermit Roosevelt Brumley (1914 - 1980) spouse - Lucille Thornbird
Avon L. Brumley (1917 - 2011) spouse - Evelyn Krahel
Doyal Wade Brumley (1920 - 2002) spouse - Lola White
William Erie Brumley (1923 - 1923) spouse - Violet Skinner
Chester Prentiss Brumley (1926 - 1978) spouse - Rachel Mann

Bessie grew up in Savannah, Tennessee. Her parents were William Payton Handley and Mary Josephine Butler.

The Handley Family
Front Row - Mamie, William Payton, Mary Josephine, Minnie, Arthur
Back Row - Russel, Bessie, Henry, Ella

Will and Bessie's three oldest children were born in Cloverdale, Lauderdale County Alabama 1904 - 1910. In 1911 their fourth child, Herbert, was born in Tishomingo county, as well as all their other children. In 1920 they were living in a new house on Mount Gilead Road near Iuka, Mississippi. This farm was their home for thirty years. It's the place they raised their children and lived until Will's death in 1950.

The Brumley's farmed their land. They raised almost everything they ate. Food was preserved to last through the winter. The smokehouse contained salt cured hams and buckets of lard. Cows furnished butter and milk. A chicken house provided eggs and fryers. Orchards provided dried fruits. Bessie made the best dried apple pies! A cellar was full of potatoes and canned jars of vegetables and berries.

They ran a general store that sat in front of their house in 1926. The name on top of the porch said "Brumley Mercantile". They stocked items for sale but they also bought farm products. Many people traded eggs or butter for items they needed such as salt, sugar, snuff, cloth, coco, or baking powder. A peddler came by each week and picked up or dropped off goods.

Every Sunday afternoon, there was a big gathering at the dog trot house on the Brumley farm. All the kids and their families were welcome to come and eat with Will and Bessie after church. They drove across the Yellow Creek bottom to attend Berea Church of Christ.

The couple worked all week preparing food for Sunday. Bessie had a wooden trunk that sat outside in the covered hallway. She kept her cakes and pies in that trunk. Sometimes she would stack 6 egg custards on top of each other and slice them. She also did sweet potato pies that way. It took more than one pie to feed this family.

On the morning of June 10, 1950. Bessie woke up to a cold house. Will always got up early. He chunked the fire in the fireplace and built a fire in the wood cook stove. Coffee was always made, and meat was sliced and ready to cook. When the house warmed up, Bessie got up, cooked biscuits and finished breakfast.

On this morning, she reached over and shook Will. "Get up old man". He called her "Old Woman" and she called him "Old Man". He was cold. Will died in his sleep.

When a person died in the fifties, their bodies were usually brought home. Families sat up with the dead. While the women stayed in the house, the men and young people stayed in the yard.

The Brumley's had nine children. Each one of them had a family of their own. By the time all the family got there, a large gathering lasted for two or three days. Friends and neighbors brought food to the house.

A long procession followed the body to the funeral. Only the children and their spouses went into the church. The church yard was full. Through open doors, they listened to the service.

After the funeral, the children and grand children took turns staying with Grandmother. There was a lot of work to be done. Animals had to be taken care of. Wood needed to be cut. Crops had to be tended and gathered.

Bessie moved into the house with her oldest daughter, Zella and Ward Parsons. She lived there until her death in 1962.

Will and Bessie Brumley's children at their mother's funeral in 1962.

Pete, Oris, Avon, Erie, Zella, Doyal, Mae, Herbert, and Kermit
Oscar Parsons, Mae Brumley Parsons, Velma Parsons, and Grandmother
Bessie Brumley

Pete Brumley

Will and Bessie's youngest son was Chester Prentiss Brumley Everyone called him "Pete".

Rachel Mann and Pete Brumley married in 1947. Rachel was the daughter of Jessie Lee Mann and Annie Osborn. Rachel's dad was a school teacher.

At the time she met Pete, Mr. Mann taught at Oak Ridge. The school was located just off of Sardis Road near the Brumley farm. James Lovelace, who was a student at Oak Ridge said the students had a special name for their teacher. It was "Mad Mann".

Jessie Mann knew that Rachel and Pete were getting too close. Rachel was just 14 years old. Her Dad really wanted his only child to get an education. That summer, he took another school, and moved his family to the Providence Community. It was near the Alabama state line, and too far for Pete to visit.

Just a couple of weeks after the move, Rachel sold her bicycle. It was a western flyer. With that money, she went to the Black and White store in Corinth. It was just across the road from the Alcorn County Courthouse. There she bought a powder blue dress with pearl buttons, and a pair of navy, open toed shoes. That was her wedding dress.

Pete borrowed his brother Kermit's car and picked her up in Corinth. He was dressed in a white shirt and grey, shark skin pants. Any time he dressed up, he always wore a white shirt. They were married at the Booneville Court House. Their next visit was to the fire tower in Blue Mountain, That's where they spent the rest of their wedding day.

Rachel told her mother about her wedding plans. She did not dare tell her father. When Lee came home, Annie told him where his daughter was. He grabbed the keys and headed out the door. Rachel was too young to get married. He was going to bring her home and have it annulled.

Just go ahead, she will run off again! You will drive her away from us if you make her choose between us and her husband. Moving forced them to marry to be together. Lee knew Annie was right. He went to bed without saying a word.

The newlyweds moved in a 2 room cabin near the Brumley farm. Pete chopped wood and stacked it under a shed. They had a fireplace and a wood cook stove. That first year, they ate a lot of rabbits. After that first year, they planted a garden and raised a pig. Rachel canned vegetables and made jellies and jam. They raised a cow and some chickens. From then on they had plenty to eat.

Will and Bessie Brumley

William Peyton Handley and Mary Josephine Butler Handley

Brumley Genealogy

William Andrew (Will) Brumley (1872-1950) (b. Burleson, Franklin Co. Ala. d. Iuka, Tishomingo Co. Ms.)
wife Bessie Handley (1884-1892) (b. Hardin Co. Tenn. d. Tishomingo Co. Ms.)

William Thomas Brumley (1820-1892) (b. Gwinnett Co. Ga. d. Franklin Co. Ala.)
wife Martha Clement (1841-1910) (b. Ga. d. Hardin Co. Tenn.)

Stephen Brumley (1795-1865) (b. South Carolina d. Marion Co. Ala.)
wife Martha Andrews (1800-1860) (b. Gwinnett Co. Ga. d. Lawrence Co. Tenn)

Stephen Brumley was one of the first settlers in Marion County, Alabama. He got a land grant for fighting in the war of 1812. He was the first Brumley in our family to move to Alabama from Georgia.

That original land grant is located in the present town of Hamilton, Alabama, near the Marion County Hospital.

Thomas Brumley (1770-1807)
wife Sarah (1771)

Handley Geneology

Bessie Leona Handley (1884-1962) (b. Olive Hill, Hardin tenn. d. Tishomingo, Ms.)
husband: William Andrew Brumley (1872-1950) (b. Burleson, Franklin Ala. d' Tishomingo, Ms.)

William Payton Handley (1843-1925) (b. Walker Ala. d. Savannah, Hardin Tenn.)
wife: Mary Josephine Butler (1857-1942) (b. Fayette, Walker Ala. d. Savannah, Hardin Tenn.)

George Thomas Handley (1819-1883) (b. Sevier, Tenn. d. Hardin, Tenn.)
wife: Mary Earnest (1821-1868) (b. Rhea, Tenn. d. Olive Hill, Hardin Tenn.)

Thomas Handley (1791-1856) (b. Washington, N.C. (Old Washington County TN.) d. Tuscaloosa, Ala.)
wife: Susan Nancy Davis (1800-1840) (b. Tenn. d. Walker, Ala.)

Sources:

Stories - Rachel Welch
Brumley stories - Velma Parsons
Story of Will's Death - Gerald Parsons

The Mann family - Big Baby Jones Hill

Jessie Lee Mann was born in Leighton, Alabama. His father was Charley Mann. His mother was Dilly Delight Cummings. Lee graduated from Leighton High School.

Dr. Montgomery of Burnsville was a family friend. His wife, once lived next door to Lee's family. The doctor said, "Burnsville needs a teacher". "If you will take a job in our county, I will help you get through school."

Money was scarce, Lee tried to work the farm. He was the only one in the family that was able to work. Financial help meant a lot to him

The doctor paid his tuition the last year of college. The Montgomery's also bought his first suit for graduation.

After getting a degree from a Bible College, he came to Tishomingo County to teach school. He spent his whole career working in this county.

In 1932, Lee married Annie Osborn. The couple had one child, Rachel Mann.

Grandpa Charley Mann was born in Cherokee County, Alabama, near Centre. Most of his family lived in Stevenson Alabama. Some of his distant family owned the Train Depot Hotel there. His mother died near Birmingham, Ala. when he was an infant. Charley raised his children in Lauderdale and Colbert County Alabama.

After Lee moved to Tishomingo County, his Mother and Dad followed him to Hubbard Salem, Providence, and Oak Ridge. They either lived in the house with him or lived near him for 25 years.

At the age of nineteen, Charley Mann married Dilly Delight Cummings. Dilly was 18.

The couple had 6 children:
Adeline Mann Huffman Cagle (1887)
Alice Mann Vandiver (1888)
Rosie Mann Young (1870-1949)
Jessie Lee Mann (1900-1949)
Rossie Mann Oswalt (1912-2002)
Samuel Mann

The 1870 census showed that Dilly lived in Houston, Winston County Alabama when she was 1 year old. Her parents were Josiah "Joe Cy" Cummings and Martha Frost Cummings.

Martha and Josiah married in 1845. They lived most of their lives in Winston County, Alabama in Littleville and Double Springs. He fought for the confederacy in the civil war. Josiah died in 1900 and is buried in Macedonia Cemetery in Needmore, Winston County Alabama. Martha moved to the Old Union Community with her daughter Agtha Haygood. At her death in 1902, she was buried at Highland Baptist Church in Tishomingo.

An article in the Mountain Eagle, March 5,1890 describes Josiah (Uncle Ci Cummings) as the mail rider from Gum Pond, Houston, and on to Double Springs, Winston County, Alabama. He rode into the Sipsy River. When he got well into it his horse stumbled and fell. The mailbags, which contained one or two registered letters was lost. After searching some distance down river, he only found his hat.

Grandma Dilly and her sister Louisa dressed in the latest fashions when they came to homecoming at Old Union. Their skirts touched the ankles. Skirt bands hugged their tiny waist. Their long hair was braided and pulled into a bun. They did not go out without a bonnet. A lady always carried a lace handkerchief.

Dilly died in 1942 at Hubbard Salem. She is buried at Old Union Cemetery. The 1930 census showed that Charlie and Dilly lived in this community. Dilly's sister, Louisa lived here. These sisters married brothers. Louisa's husband was Henry Mann. Charlie's father, William Evan Mann, and several member's of the Mann family lived in the Old Union Community.

Their Grandson, Carl Huffman, had lived with them until 1942. He joined the army in World War II. All of their children were grown and married. Samuel, his youngest son died at the age of 17. For the first time in his life, Grandpa Charley was alone.

Rachel, his granddaughter remembers the day he married his 2nd wife, Miss Ida.

"Grandpa's New Wife"

It was a Saturday morning. Rachel and Lee were in Iuka. More people went to town on Saturday than any other day of the week. Almost all the parking spaces in front of the stores were full. Lee parked on the other side of the street. He sold McNess products out of the trunk of his car. His best selling products were vanilla flavoring and red lineament.

They usually spent most of the day in Iuka. Rachel liked to walk up the street and look at all the decorated store windows. She always met someone to hang out with. They usually went to the movie theater, walked to the park, or got a fountain coke at the drug store.

While walking to the court house, a Trailway bus passed her. Rachel ran to tell Lee that she saw Grandpa riding on a bus. That's probably someone that looks like Grandpa. Lee drove from Iuka to Hubbard Salem every week to check on Grandpa. He did not say anything about going to see his kids. Besides, they always picked him up. He did not have the money to take bus trips. The bus station was at a gas station near Mineral Springs Park. That's where you went to buy a ticket. Grandpa was not there. They drove back to town. Grandpa got off the bus on main street in Iuka. He had a suitcase in his hand and a woman by his side.

When we walked up to them, Grandpa said, "Lee and Rachel, this is my wife Ida." Ida meet my son and granddaughter. Grandpa seemed to be talking to me. He did not look at Lee. He asked if we could give them a ride home. Without saying a word, Lee loaded the suitcase in the car. Rachel and Grandpa Charley did most of the talking on the way home. Miss Ida said a few words. Lee never opened his mouth.

Grandpa had been writing to Miss Ida Grey. She was from Ash Ridge, a community near Double Springs, Alabama. One of his granddaughters married Miss Ida's brother. They introduced the couple.

I guess Lee got over his mad spell. A few weeks later he moved Grandpa and Miss Ida in the house with him. In 1948, Lee and Annie built a new house in Iuka. It was located on highway 72. A well known fish restaurant is located on the site today. The house was located at the top of Big Baby Jones Hill. The family converted a garage that was located on the property into a small house. Lee and Annie lived here while they built their new house. Grandpa and Miss Ida moved there after the new house was completed.

While living in the garage, Lee and Annie walked down the hill in back of their house to a spring. They carried water from this spring until a well was dug at their new house. Lee set up a big black wash pot near the spring. He kept plenty of kindling and short sticks of wood. a shed was built to keep the wood dry. This was named the wash house. That's where Annie would heat water in the wash pot, and wash their clothes. Lee also put up a clothes line near the wash pot. With a long wooden paddle, the clothes were lifted out of the hot water, rinsed in a tub of cold water, and hung to dry on the clothes line.

The dry clothes were carried to the house where they were starched and ironed. Starch was made by pouring a powder into a pot of water. Items such as handkerchiefs, blouses, and dresses were soaked in starch. Occasionally curtains, tablecloths, pillowcases, and doilies were starched. After the starched clothes dried they were ironed. This gave them a smooth, crisp look.

Occasionally Rachel did a big wash for her elderly neighbor, Mrs. Gilcrist. She paid her by the piece. 10 cents for handkerchiefs and small items. She got a half dollar to wash, starch, and iron a big item like a tablecloth.

Rachel spent her wash money by ordering something from the Sears Catalog. Most of her children's clothes were sewed at home. It was nice to get something store bought to add to their wardrobe. She liked to buy patent leather shoes, lace socks, plastic diaper covers, and hair barrettes. During the fifties, electric appliances started making these household chores much easier. An electric washing machine sat on their covered back porch. That stopped most of the trips to the wash house

Charley Hampton Mann

Whitfield Mann Family

Jessie Lee Mann

Mann genealogy

Jessie Lee Mann (1900-1949) (b. Leighton, Colbert Co. Ala. d. Iuka, Ms.)
wife Annie Osborn (1904-1973) (b. Short, Tishomingo Co. Ms. d. Iuka, Ms.)

Charlie Hampton Mann (1867-1963) (b. Centre, Cherokee Co. Ala. d. Double Springs, Winston Co. Ala.)
wife Lolita Delitha Adelia (Dilly Delite) Cummings (1868-1942) (b. Houston, Winston Co. Ala. d. Tishomingo Co. Ms.)

Whitfield Evan Mann (1837-1920) (b. Abbeville, S.C. d. Cloverdale, Lauderdale Co. Ala.) A Confederate soldier. Buried Mann family cemetery, Valley, Ms.
wife Mary Jane Lamberth (1828-1870) (b. Sallacoa, Cherokee Co. Georgia d. Jefferson Co. Ala.)

Aman A. Mann (1817-1862) (b. Newberry, S.C. d. Vicksburg Ms.) A Confederate soldier killed at Vicksburg.
wife Mary Lockridge (1835-1905) (Abbeville S.C. d. Brownwood, Texas)

Manassah Mann (1782-1817)(b. Newberry S.C. d. S.C.)
wife RachelDavenport (1782-1824) (b.

Cummings genealogy

Lolita Delita Adelia Cummings (b. June 1868, ala. d. 1942 Tishomingo Co., Ms. Buried Old Union Cemetery)
husband: Charley Mann (1867-1963)

Josiah Cummings (b. 8 April, 1826. Marion Ala. d. 1900 Winston Ala.)
Martha E. Frost (b. 1826 Ala. d. 9 Apr. 1902 Tishomingo County, Old Union Cemetery)

CHAPTER 7

OSBORN FAMILY - THE POWHATAN

William Riley (Billy) Osborn came to Tishomingo County in 1880. Born in Laurens S.C., He was the son of Langston Osborn and Mary Little.

On June 3, 1836 William enlisted in the 3 Brig. Georgia Militia (Infantry). His Company was called the Fayette Blues under the command of Colonel William Wood in the Creek Indian War. For his service, William received two land grants for a total of 120 acres.

He married Susan Magby Holcomb in Winston Co. Ala. in November,1851. Together they had 11 children.

Mary Ellen Osborn (1852-1919)
Mary Elizabeth "Molly" (1854-1930)
Elizabeth Osborn (1855-1930)
William Langston" Bud" Osborn (1858-1932)
Serena Osborn (1859-1930)
Susan Osborn (1862-1880)
Rhoda Osborn (1862-1934)
Jonathan Osborn "Jot"(1866-1921)

Samuel Thomas Osborn (1867-1937)
John H. Osborn (1870- 1915)
Martha A. "Mattie" Osborn (1872-1938)
Nancy Lou Sarah "Nan" Osborn (1875-1956)

All of their children were born in Alabama, except for their youngest
daughter. Nancy Osborn was born in Tishomingo County, Ms.
He was a charter member of the New Salem Church in Iuka, Miss.
That's where he chose to be buried in 1900

William Riley Osborn and Susan Magby Holcomb Family

"The Indian Princess"

Not long ago, Annie Osborn's great grand kids were in a theater
production of "Pocahontas". Their grandmother said "Hey, you may
be playing the part of your own ancestors." You did not descend from
Pocahontas, but there is a blood tie to her family.

In 1619, a 32 year old soldier named Thomas Osborn, sailed from
London, England to the Virginia Colony. He was hired to serve in

the military, which protected a large track of college land (10,000 acres) at Henrico.

In 1618 royal charter was obtained to build a proposed school to educate the Indians in Christianity, and to provide the planter's children with advanced tuition. This would have been the college of William and Mary. Plans for the first college in America were canceled in 1622.

In March of that year, Indians attacked and killed many settlers. Lieutenant Thomas Osborn led a successful retaliatory attack on the Indians. After that, he became Captain Thomas Osborn. This group of men were credited with keeping the colony from being eradicated in the massacre of 1622.

For his service, Thomas received 500 acres of land, located on the south side of the James River. In 1625, he moved there and built the Coxendale Plantation. It became a center for shipping and grading tobacco.

Thomas lived his entire life at Coxendale, as well as the next 5 generations of his namesake.

Thomas Osborn V was the first Osborn to leave Coxendale. He married Anne Worsham in 1714. They moved to CharlotteCounty Virginia, and bought 400 acres of land from Thomas Jefferson's father, Peter Jefferson. They later sold most of the land and opened a tavern. Thomas and Anne are buried at the Charlotte Court House in Union Cemetery.

Many Tishomingo County Osborns descended from Thomas and Anne's son, Daniel. He was born in 1730 in Henrico. Daniel served as a private in the South Carolina Continental line during the Revolutionary War. After the war he received a land grant and moved to Laurens South Carolina.

100 years before Anne and Thomas married, Anne's great grand father came to Virginia as an indentured servant. In this colony, tobacco was the most profitable crop. It required labor to operate the plantations. If a person agreed to work three years on a plantation, they received passage to Virginia and fifty acres of land.

A few years after his arrival, George married an Indian princess, Her father was Wahunsenacawh, a Powhatan Chief of thirty districts and one hundred fifty villages. He had twenty six children who were half siblings. One of the half sisters was Pocahontas. I don't know George's wife's Indian name. She took the English name Susannah. Like Pocahontas, (Rebecca) she became a christian and wore English clothes.

George married his wife in 1619, during a time of good relation between the settlers and the Indians. This peace started in 1614, when John Rolfe married Pocahontas. It lasted about 8 years. The Powhatan Chief had a connection to the English village by having a child living there. That was the way he connected to many of the villages he ruled. He had twenty six children from different villages.

John Rolfe and Pocahontas lived in an area called the Bermuda 100. Established in 1613, just six years after the first Virginia settlement of Jamestown in 1607. It lay where the James and the Appomattox rivers converged. George and Susannah also lived here.

Indians had occupied this area for 10,000 years. A group of settlers worked together to form a plantation. it was called !00 that group of settlers could number up to 100.

The Powhatan chief gave Pocahontas a large tract of land called the Varina Plantation. John Rolfe may have grown the first marketable tobacco here, where he lived with his wife from 1614-1619. Their son Thomas Rolfe was born here in 1615.

Several generations of the Worsham family also owned land in the Bermuda 100. Some descended from George, others came from England and settled here. Some married into the Epps family.

George and Susannah only saw three years of good relations between the colonist and the Indians. Her sister, Pocahontas, died the year of their marriage, 1619. Her father, the Powhatan chief, died a year later. A new chief took charge. He had no tolerance for the persecution of his people. As more settlers moved in, the good relations deteriorated.

In 1622, an effort was made to wipe out the colony. The Indians came to the settlers as they worked. They pretended to be friends bearing gifts. All the plantations from Jamestown to Henrico were attacked. 347 of the 1,250 settlers were killed in the massacre 1622. George and Susannah were two of only forty settlers left alive in the Bermuda 100.

They had 2 children. One was born in 1622, the other in 1624. I could not find anything written about the Indian Princess, after the massacre.

Osborn genealogy

Samuel Thomas Osborn (1867-1937) (b. Chalk Bluff, Marion Co. Al. d. Tishomingo Co. Ms.) wife: Minnie Tennessee Jane Brown. (1882-1913) (b. and d. Short, Tishomingo Co. Ms.)

William Riley Osborn (Billy) (1811-1900) (b. Laurens, SC d. Iuka, Tishomingo Co. Ms.)
wife: Susan Magby Holcomb (1833-1911) (b. DeKalb, Ga. d. Tishomingo Co. Ms.)

Langston Osborn (1780-1833) (b. SC) wife: Mary Little (1787-1870) (b. Edgefield SC. d. Tishomingo Co. Ms.)

Daniel Osborn (1730-1826) (b. Henrico, Va. d. Laurens, SC.) wife: Margaret Stout (1744-1805) (b. York, Pa. d. Orange, NC)

Thomas Osborne IV (1690-1755) (b. Henrico, Va. d. Lunnenberg, Va.) wife: Anne Worsham (1665-1739) (b. and d. Henrico, Va.)

Thomas Osborne III (1641-1692) (b. Henrico, Va. d. Chesterfield, Va.) wife: Sisely Bailey
(1641-1686) (b. and d. Henrico, Va.)

Source:

1870 US Census Thorn Hill, Marion Co. Ala.
1880 US Census Tishomingo County, Ms.
An article written by Bonnie Gober, a descendant of William Riley Osborn.

Annie and Willie Carlisle

Annie Osborn Mann married Willie Carlisle in 1954. He was her second husband, and she was his second wife. They married later in life. Willie and Sinai Moore had the following children:

Ethel Carlisle husband Luther Luttrel
Willie Jesse (W J) Carlisle wife Alice Lewis
Clifford Carlisle wife Onita Woodruff (Tootsie)
Lora Faye Carlisle husband JD Grisham
Clarence Carlisle

Annie only had one child, Rachel Welch,

In the 50's and early 60's, I loved to visit my grand parents. They lived in a large white house that once had a dog trot between the two front rooms. A fireplace heated each room. If they knew we were coming, Mr. Carlisle built a fire. They only built a fire in the room they slept in if they did not have company. Each room contained two beds. Flannel blankets served as sheets.

A few times we got there late. Maw maw Annie tucked us in with our clothes on. She piled so many quilts on us we could not even wiggle. The next morning we gathered in front of the fireplace, waiting on the call that breakfast was ready.

A mantle clock struck each hour. It chimed six times. They got up early.

When they were working in the fields, breakfast was the only time they cooked. There was two pans of biscuits and a platter full of meat. We had eggs with red - eye gravy, home made butter, and blackberry jam. For dinner and supper Maw Annie just added something like fried sweet potatoes or sorghum molasses. She already had the meat and bread cooked. They drank Louisiana Coffee for breakfast. For all the other meals we drank fresh milk.

Maw Annie milked every day. I think she was glad to raise a calf, just to take a break from milking.

A few times I picked blackberries in Bolton's Bottom. Maw Annie picked enough to make plenty of jam. I was usually covered in chiggers. When we got home, I had to take a bath in the tub. The tub was plumbed to take the water out, but we did not have water in the house. Usually she filled a washpan with warm water. a kettle on the fireplace always held hot water. With a wash rag and a small piece of lye soap, we got a bath before we went to bed at night.

I loved to gather eggs. slop the pigs, and watch as the cow was milked. my grand parents raised cotton, corn, and sorghum molasses. They used a red farmal tractor to tend the crops. Cotton was their money crop. A patch of corn was raised to feed the animals.

The sorghum produced a couple gallons of molasses for their own table, they sold what was left to friends and neighbors. I remember getting $6.00 for a metal gallon bucket of molasses. Mr. Oscar Johnson always bought molasses from me. I loved to deliver them to him.

One fall, I helped harvest the sorghum. With a wooden paddle we stripped the leaves from the stalk. The leaves were tied in bundles. They were stored in the barn for fodder, which was fed to the cows in the winter. I cut the stalk with a machete knife and loaded it on the back of a pickup truck. Now it was ready for the sorghum mill. Mr. Dean operated a mill in the Harmony community.

We had to wait in a long line, the mill only operated at harvest time. The molasses had to be made while the fires were hot. Stalks were fed through a press that mashed the syrup into a hot vat. Wood was burned under the vat until the syrup thickened into molasses. A faucet was turned and hot molasses filled gallon buckets. I was cautioned not to get too close. There were many ways to get burned. Yellow jackets swarmed those sugary vats. No one had to tell me to stay away from them.

Patsy was Mr. Carlisle's grand daughter. Since we were the same age, my grand parents let us visit at the same time. We also worked together. We hoed cotton in the spring. and picked cotton in the fall. I am sure they paid us more than what we were worth. My Grandparents wanted to teach us how to work. They did not give us money. We had to do chores for every cent we received.

"Extracting the Pea"

One day, Patsy and I were shelling peas on the front porch. Being silly, I put two peas in my nostrils. I guess I breathed in instead of out, because one of the peas went up my nose.

I did not tell anyone, not even Patsy. I knew she would tell Maw Annie and they would get that pea out by what ever means it took. You see they usually did their own doctoring. If I could not reach it, I figured they would have to cut a hole in my face to get it out.

It stayed in there over night. Patsy and I slept in the same bed. I guess she thought I had to go to the bathroom a lot, but I was outside blowing my nose.

The next day, I told Patsy I was probably going to die. I could not survive the pain of being cut. Being the good friend she was, Patsy did not tell on me.

She said there's got to be a way to get that pea. She rolled a piece of paper and tried to suck it out. That did not work. She said, "We have to stop up all the holes". Patsy placed her fingers in my ears, Placing my finger in the right nostril, I blew hard as I could. The pea blew out. I have never been as relieved as I was that day.

My grandparents did a lot of fun things with us while we stayed with them. Every fall they took us to Corinth to buy our school clothes. We had to spend our cotton money, but we got to buy anything we wanted to wear. My mom would not let me do that.

They also took us to the fair in Corinth each fall, after we finished picking cotton. We always visited a big flea market at Ripley, Ms. It was held the first of each month. Ma Annie never left the house without milk jugs of frozen water. The trip to Ripley took a full day. We left before daylight and did not get back until after dark. A slug burger, pecan pie, and coke was our usual lunch. Maw Annie always brought plenty of food. It was usually biscuits and meat from breakfast. She also made a dried apple pie for each one of us. We usually stopped and snacked along the road.

Another adventure we shared with my grand parents was a trip to Pine Flats to look for deer tracks. Mr. Carlisle loved to deer hunt. I don't think there was as many deer in Tishomingo County sixty years ago as there are today. The first deer I remember seeing was a dead one in the back of a pick-up truck. You did not see them wandering around in someone's yard like you do now. They had a very short hunting season. It was usually around Thanksgiving and Christmas. We would look for tracks before the season began. That way he would have his hunting spot picked out and ready for the season to begin.

CHAPTER 8

RACHEL'S FAMILY

Rachel Mann married Pete Brumley in 1947. Their children were:
Betty Brumley (Compton)
Nelda Brumley (Belue)
Shirley Brumley (Embry)
Stanley Brumley

The Brumley Children - Nelda, Shirley, Betty, and Stanley

Pete and Rachel lived in the house with Rachel's mother, Annie. Annie's husband, Jessie Lee Mann died in September of 1949. Rachel was pregnant with their first child. When Lee got sick with Leukemia. Rachel and Pete moved in to help care for her father.

The Brumley children were all born in a bungalow house that overlooked hwy 72, just as you entered the town of Iuka. It sat at the top of Big Baby Jones Hill.

Porches spanned the front and back of this brown, brick siding house. For water, the family lowered a bucket into a well that stood on the back porch. Out back stood a chicken house, which also served as the family out house.

Doctor Collum delivered Betty in the back bedroom on January 5, 1950. A week later, an ice storm hit Tishomingo county. Electricity was out for 12 days. The family stayed warm because they had wood heat. Dad always kept a stack of dry wood on the back porch. Everything in the yard was covered in ice. Popping sounds were loud as a gun shot. Tree limbs were snapping from the weight of the ice. They had light from the fireplace and coal oil lamps. The electricity was off for two weeks. Maw Annie always kept the lamps filled, just in case of an emergency. She also had plenty of food that she had canned.

Momma worried that her newborn could get sick or that she could have complications from the birth. There's no way a doctor could get over those roads.

Our family lived here until Betty was five years old. Her best friend was Jimmy Seago. These two spent a lot of time sitting on the road bank watching cars go by.

The Seagos were our neighbors. They got a tv before we did. On Saturdays, they invited me to watch. The first show I remember seeing was "The Lone Ranger." I also liked "Howdy Doody".

My Mom and Dad got so tired of hearing, "It's Howdy Doody" time. "It's Howdy Doody Time."

Another playmate was Barbara Ray. Her Dad, Leonard Ray, owned a garage across the highway from our house. Sometimes he walked her across the road to play with little Betty. Mud pies were our favorite thing to make. Once we picked all of Maw Annie's carnations to decorate our pies. Barbara learned a new song, "Bimbo" We sang as we baked. We had red clay from our head to our toes.

Betty was a teenager in the sixties. On November 22, 1963 she stood at her locker in the hallway of Iuka school, when she heard President Kennedy had been shot.

"Iuka Drive-In"

If you went on a date in Tishomingo County, it was probably to a ballgame, church, or a drive-in movie. The Iuka Drive-in was always full on Saturday nights. Teens always parked on the back row. Families with younger kids parked on the front and middle rows.

Everyone went to the concession stand at intermission. One light bulb glowed over the door. You had to go to the concession stand to see who was there and to be seen.

Bobby asked me to go to the Drive-in with him. One of those Beach Party movies with Annette Funicello and Frankie Avalon was playing. I was fifteen. Bobby was in a grade above me, He was sixteen and went to a different school. I had never been on a movie date. Group activities like bowling, ballgames, or church were not real dates.

I was surprised that my Mom said "yes" when I asked to go. His parents were her best friends and neighbors when both couples were newlyweds.

Bobby was cute! I was eager to drive around Jack and Jill with him. That was the teen hangout. It was not nearly as cool to be there without a date. If my parents drove me there, I slid down in the seat where no one would recognize me.

Bobby came in and talked to my parents. My dad, had to tease him. He said," You are not the same guy who was here last Saturday night."

He also showed him his military picture and bragged, "After years of practice, I am a pretty good shot." Then he got very serious and said, "Don't you be doing any of that drag racing with her in the car, and be home by 11."

We sat on a pickup tailgate and talked to friends that gathered during the first half of the movie. He brought us popcorn, cokes, and hotdogs. I was impressed that he spent so much money on me. Mom gave me money to buy my own food.

The second half of the movie began, and the crowd dwindled. Everyone went to their own cars.

This handsome guy put his arm around my shoulder. My heart was fluttering. I slid a little closer to him. Oh, he smelled so good. Some kind of hair oil made his hair black and shiny. I think he was going for the Elvis look.

With only the flickering light from the movie, everything was magical. Both of us were still and quiet. He touched my neck with his fingertip.

All at once white teeth glared and he came at me with a vampire growl. Scrambling for the car door, I tried to escape. He was too close, I slugged him with all the force I could put into my right fist.

Bobby kept saying," I am sorry! I did not mean to scare you! I was just kidding! I think he was just trying to get up the courage to kiss me.

I said, "Take me home." If I take you home now, James and Rachel will drag me out of this car. We decided to go to Jack and Jill until 11.

I was sorry that I hit him. He did not let on, but I knew it must have hurt. The next day at school, Bobby had a black eye. He also had a cut, my birthstone ring had scratched his cheek.

He told his classmates, a cow kicked him, while he was cleaning the stall. Bobby and I were always good friends, but he never asked me to go on another date.

"We got married in a snow storm"

Betty Brumley married Harvey Compton December 23, 1966. The couple planned to marry while school was out for Christmas holidays. Betty was still a student at Iuka High School. Plans were made for the two families to meet at the East Corinth Church of Christ. The minister had been Harvey's preacher, when he was a young boy.

About an hour before the wedding, it started snowing. The accumulation was fast and heavy. The families could not drive in bad weather. They said, "You have to put off this wedding". Betty's comeback was, "I am getting married, even if I have to hitch a ride on a snow plough. The trip to the church was slow, but they got there without sliding off the road.

The preacher, who worked for the railroad in Corinth, had been called in to work. He thought the wedding would be postponed. His wife had an emergency number to get a hold of him. "They drove through a snow storm to get here. You need to take off work and marry them." She signed the wedding certificate as a witness, but she did not leave the house. The church was just across the street.

After a short, but beautiful ceremony, they walked into a winter wonderland. The car was covered with snow. Preacher Case drove the newly weds to the nearest motel, which was the Corona Plaza. He was driving a railroad truck with chains. Honeymoon plans were to drive to the Thunderbird, in Jackson, Tn. Oh Well! At least they did not have to stay with the preacher!

Harvey and Betty Brumley Compton

The Burnsville Train Depot

CHAPTER 9

SKIRMISHES AT GLENDALE AND BURNSVILLE

As I was searching for information about my ancestors, I read an article that mentioned a civil war battle in Burnsville, Mississippi. I was not familiar with any fighting that took place here, but I knew it was all around us. I was interested because Burnsville is my home town.

A Union soldier with the 1st Alabama Cavalry gave this account of the Battle of Burnsville.

On April 13, 1863, Johnny's attacked the Union camp at Glendale. The guards for the day had just reported to headquarters to be assigned to their post. Firing began. All of the troops were ordered out by the regimental bugler blowing "Boots and Saddle". Two well directed shots from a 12 pounder blew up the ammunition sheds. Colonel Morrill, the commander of the post telegraphed General Dodge, "Under attack, the strength of the enemy unknown".

Troops from the 1st Alabama Cavalry charged out on them. Finding a small squad, they drove them back to Burnsville.

The last line of the day was formed on a hill about a mile west of the village. From that position, we could see the Johnnys in Burnsville. They were too numerous for us to attack. These troops were Roddy's men, a Confederate Brigadier General who defended areas near the Tennessee River.

While we watched the Johnnies, Colonel Cornyn arrived from Corinth with the 10th Missouri, 15th Illinois, and 8th Michigan Cavalry. They brought a battery of four 12 pounder mountain howitzers.

The 1st Alabama Cavalry was ordered back to our camp at Glendale, which was eight miles away, for rations and ammunition. On the way back, we met the 7th and 9th Illinois infantry. Each one wanted to know where the Johnnys were. "There is a considerable force in Burnsville." During the day, several regiments of the 16th infantry also marched out of Corinth.

On April 14,1863, the 1st Alabama Cavalry joined the other troops at Burnsville and the battle began. We came fighting hard. Roddy's men were known for quick skirmishes. Hit and run. It was rumored that these attacks were a ploy to detain the 16th infantry and keep them from Eastport. The next morning, the 1st Alabama Cavalry was in the front line that marched through Iuka and on to Eastport.

Troops traveled from Glendale on a road that wound through Burnsville, crossed Yellow Creek on Turnpike Mountain Road, and passed Harmony Baptist Church. They passed Iuka Cemetery, marched through Iuka and on to Eastport Road.

Evidence of fighting has been found on the hill overlooking Burnsville. Stonewall Compton lived on this hill. He uncovered mini balls each spring when he plowed his truck patches. He had a shoe box full of civil war ammunition.

On December 14,1899, the National Tribune published an article that described the civil war action of the 1st Alabama Cavalry Union regiment. It was raised from Alabama Unionist in October of 1862. Their duties consisted of scouting, flank guard, and providing screening to the infantry, for the union troops that occupied the area along the Tennessee River in Mississippi and Alabama 1862 - 1864. From the camp at Glendale, Mississippi, the Federal troops saw action in Cherokee, Barton Station, Tuscumbia, Eastport, and Jasper, Alabama.

Several members of my daddy's family, the Brumley's, joined the 1st Alabama Cavalry. The 17 year old union soldier who gave an account of the Battle of Burnsville was Pinkney Hall. His father William A. Hall's second wife was Almedia Brumley. Two other Brumley sisters had husbands in the 1st Alabama Cavalry, Peter Lewis and Wesley Williams. All were stationed at Glendale. These families were all neighbors in the Bull Mountain area of Franklin County, Alabama.

On April 15, 1863, the same day as the battle at Burnsville. Sarah Brumley's husband, Peter Lewis died in the post hospital at Corinth. The cause of death was listed as continual fever. Brothers Riley and Barton Brumley enlisted in Company B of the 1st Alabama Union Calvary in Glendale, Alcorn County Mississippi. In 1862 Company B was enlisting. Recruits filled Company B, C, and D. There were enough soldiers to form two battalions.

A Divided Family

Like many families in Mississippi and Alabama, the Brumley's were divided in their support of the Union and the Confederacy. This conflict ripped families and communities apart. Brothers, William Thomas and David Brumley joined the Confederacy. Riley and Barton Brumley joined the Union.

It was not only the military men that had to make a choice. There was not one person that was not affected by the war, everyone had to choose a side. Neighbors and family members turned on each other.

What made them choose the cause that many would be asked to give their life for? Much depended on how each person was affected by the war.

Although it was not the only reason, many joined for economic reasons. The war not only affected the price of cotton, Mississippi's biggest crop. It reached all areas of the economy. Most trade and commerce ceased.

The sawmills at Burnsville were shut down following secession. A company of Burnsville volunteers joined the confederacy at Glendale in May of 1861. Known as "The Burnsville Blues", most had worked at the area sawmills. The Confederate army was the only option for employment in this area.

Many probably did not realize what would be required of them as soldiers. They had no way of knowing what was coming to this area.

Battle of Shiloh - April 6-7, 1862
Siege of Corinth- April 29-May 30, 1862
Battle of Iuka - September 19, 1862
Battle of Corinth October 3-4, 1862

Micajah D. Moreland of the "Burnsville Blues" commanded the 17th Mississippi Regiment Company E. It was later designated Captain Moreland's Company. On September 7,1862, William Henry Blakney, a Burnsville recruit, that followed Captain Moreland to a new command. They formed Company C of Roddy's 4th Alabama Confederate Cavalry Regiment.

Thomas Young from Coles Mill enlisted in Moreland's Alabama Cavalry Company G on July 1,1863. This Confederate Battalion was raised in Russelville, Alabama, with men from Franklin County. Assigned to General Roddy's 4th Brigade, the Company was involved in skirmishes in North Alabama in the winter and spring of 1864. They moved to Mississippi, where they took an active part in the fighting at Tishomingo Creek (Brice's Crossroads). On May 18, 1865 the Company surrendered at Iuka, Mississippi. Thomas Young is buried in the Hubbard Salem Cemetery in Tishomingo County, Mississippi.

Two other family members from Tishomingo County fought in the Confederate Cavalry Regiment. David Reeder Hubbard was a Captain in the 1st Alabama Cavalry. He enlisted December 17, 1861. Ruben Rufus Marlar served in the Tennessee 12 Cavalry Company E. John W. Blakney served in Company E, Mississippi Jeff Davis Cavalry.

Robert A. Moore kept a war diary. In it, he documented the trip by rail of the 17th Mississippi Regiment from Corinth, Mississippi to Manassas, Virginia. Company F was made up of men from his hometown, Burnsville, Mississippi. The train left Corinth on June 12, 1861. It took an hour and a half for the train to travel the twelve mies from Corinth to Burnsville.

In 1860, Burnsville was a booming town. The railroad and sawmills were responsible for most of the economic boom. The First Methodist Church had a large congregation. Pine log houses, were the homes of many mill workers. Several mercantile provided goods and services for the mill workers.

All over the south, people were divided about secession. From the feelings of my family, I determined these views. Some wanted to secede, others wanted to save the union. Most people that wanted to save the union lived in the mountainous areas of the South. They worked small farms and did not own slaves. They did not want their government to change. They did not feel that they would have equal representation in a government controlled by rich land owners. In 1860, many would have voted to keep the union.

The other group included the planters, who had to have slave labor to operate their plantations. They saw Lincoln's election as a threat to their property. They wanted a government that would protect their way of life. The state should have more control. That would give them a bigger voice in their government.

Because of its small farms, and river trade with the North, Tishomingo County was one of the few counties in Mississippi that did not vote to secede. Although they supported the rule of the majority after Mississippi seceded, Many joined the Confederacy, even though they had not been for secession. Not everyone in the south was for the Confederacy at that time.

Every state had Union supporters. Mississippi did not have the division that Alabama had, because almost all of its counties were plantation areas. The state of Virginia divided because of the different views of the mountain people and the planters.

Why did William Thomas and David Henry Brumley choose the Confederacy? They lived at Nauvoo, Alabama in an area of larger farms. They were feeling the economic collapse after secession.

They did not see the Confederacy as the offensive guerilla's that fought and killed their families at Bull Mountain. They now saw them as defenders of the South.

An invading army of northern soldiers were on their way. The best way to defend their homes, and protect the south was to have a united army of defenders. That's why most southerners joined the confederacy. They fought to defend their family and home. Even the ones that were not for secession saw the need to defend themselves. They now had a cause they believed in and a reason to fight.

A soldier named William Brumley fought in the Battle of Shiloh. His regiment was the first to attack the union forces. William Brumley was shot in the left arm. He was sent to a hospital in Corinth. After that he was absent from duty.

I did not find any documented proof that this was my grandfather. He was older than his three younger brothers that fought in the civil war.

We know he supported the confederate side. A description of his body states he had a crippled arm. Family stories say, They tried to cut off his arm and he ran away.

The main treatment for an infected wound during the Battle of Shiloh was amputation. Being alert enough to know what was about to happen, he ran away from the hospital. His arm could be saved if he could find someone to doctor his wounds. A sister, Amanda Lambert, lived in Iuka at the time. She may have helped him.

Phillip Dale Roddy, Brigadier General CSA, was charged with defending the area along the Tennessee River in northeast Mississippi and north Alabama. The General was born in Moulton, Alabama in 1826.

As a young man, he bought a steamship that docked at Eastport. He might have fought for the Union, especially because he did so much business with the north. His boat hauled goods from Illinois to Eastport. Roddy burned his boat. The Union army was going to use it to attack ports along the river. Roddy joined the Confederacy. He gathered a group of men and fought his first battle at Shiloh.

Why did the Brumley's from Bull Mountain choose to fight for the Union? In Winston County, a group of county officials passed an amendment concerning the war. They wanted to remain neutral, they would not bear arms against their friends and neighbors.

They did not believe secession from the union was legal. If the state could secede from the country, than the county of Winston would secede from the state. Many of their forefathers had fought to establish a country with rights and freedoms for all of its citizens. They did not trust a new government to protect those rights.

In Alabama, a strip of land from Tuscumbia to Huntsville was the best land for cotton plantations. This area was the source of most of the state's wealth in 1860. Many thought the large land owners of Alabama, overstepped their power when they voted to secede. They controlled the state government because most of the senators and representatives were wealthy land owners. The ones that represented the poorer districts were pressured into voting to secede. Some were even thrown in jail until they changed their vote. Their vote did not represent their district's choice. People from the mountain areas were losing their voice in the government.

In 1860, most of the people were not that concerned with the war. Within a year every thing changed. Everyone was forced to make a choice. Their decision was made depending on how the war affected their families. The following are some factors that determined this family's choice.

Recruiters from both sides were enlisting soldiers. A rally for CSA was held at Pikesville, A ghost town just south of Hamilton, Alabama. In 1860 it was the county seat. William Hall and several others refused to take down the American flag that flew over the post office. They used guns to back off the mob. From then on, they were known as leaders of the opposition. They did not know or care anything about the Yankees. They were just defending the flag that they were raised to respect. These confederate sympathizers were burning American flags to rally people to their cause.

You had to be careful what you said. Both sides were volatile. Some people were beaten, a few were killed, just because they spoke out about the war.

The Halls, as well as others, were forced to leave their homes in Marion County. They moved to Bull Mountain to live next to the Brumley's. This area of the mountains was sparsely settled. Pinkney Hall's step-mother was Riley and Barton Brumley's sister. It was peaceful for over a year. Neither side bothered the people of Bull Mountain until 1863.

The state of Alabama passed a draft that required hundreds of young men from each county to enlist in the confederacy. When the counties did not meet their quotas, they were counted as traitors. They were willing to overlook the charges if the boys enlisted in the confederate army.

Montgomery ordered the local guard (300 soldiers) to wipe out the union sympathizers. This put brother against brother, family against family, and friends and neighbors against each other.

This is where the term guerrilla warfare came from. Crops were destroyed, animals slaughtered, houses were burned. Many were forced to live in caves and hide out in the Freedom Hills. Many atrocities were committed against the residents of five Alabama counties: Winston, Franklin, Walker, Marion, and Fayette.

I read about many mutilations and killings, but I am only going to tell about what happened to my family.

Charles Cagle, who was part of the Cummings family was killed by the home guard in October of 1863. He lived in Cagle Cove near the Natural Bridge. His father, Henry Cagle was the first man to get a land grant in Winston County in 1836.

One night, a band of about thirty armed men rode to their farm. They hung Charles and his fifteen year old son. After the men left, their mother cut the rope that was around their neck. The young boy survived, but his father did not. The Cagles fled Winston County, and went to Giles, Tennessee.

The new government in Montgomery thought that by dealing harshly with a few. It would cause the others to enlist. That did not happen. Instead it pushed them to the Union side.

This is Pinkney Hall's account of what happened when the guerrillas came to Bull Mountain in 1863. They first came to Wesley Williams house. Shots were fired and their house was burned. Next they came to the Brumley house. They exchanged fire, but no one was killed.

Hearing the shots gave the Halls a little warning. Pinkney and his father, William started running. They really wanted to capture William, who they considered to be a leader.

Bloodhounds were set on their trail. The dogs were getting closer. William said, "Go on son, I am going to slow you down". Just about the time we were ready to give up, a creek came into view. The dogs lost our scent as we ran up the creek. Cold and wet, we crawled into a high cave. That's where we hid until dark. The guerrillas would not stay in the hills after dark.

Some hill people were confederate, others were for the union, but they were loyal to each other first. There were friends from both sides that helped us. We could not go home. Women slipped into the hills and brought us food and clothing. We joined others that had been run from their homes. Many barely survived without food, guns, and warm clothing.

The best way they could fight back was to join the union army. They had been forced to make a choice. They would fight to save the union.

A group of twenty men followed Bear Creek until we met a union scout. He mapped out a trail for us to take. The main roads were guarded. By following the North Star and traveling at night, we made our way to Glendale, Mississippi. There we enlisted in the 1st Alabama Cavalry Company B.

Pinkney Hall was just a boy of 16 years of age when he enlisted in the 1st Alabama Cavalry. His father, who was with him, thought he would be safer in the military than he would have been back in Franklin County.

About 2,500 men from Winston, Marion, Franklin, Fayette, and Walker Counties, Alabama joined the 1st Alabama Cavalry in the Union Army. At Glendale they saw the first blue uniforms they had ever laid eyes on.

The civil war split families apart all over the south. A feud developed between the Marlar and Lambert families in Burnsville that lasted for generations. James Monroe Lambert left his mule tied up in the field and joined the Union army with the 1st Alabama Cavalry. His mother's brother, Joseph Marlar joined the Confederate army.

The civil war is the reason many family members moved to Tishomingo County. The Compton's lived in Dallas, Georgia. After Sherman's army marched through Georgia and burned their farm, they bought land in Lawrence County, Alabama and later moved to Burnsville.

Many soldiers could not return to their homes after the war. Others left because they saw new places. Some did not have a home or family to go home too. Some of the Brumley's went to Texas and Missouri after the war. The two brothers that fought for the Union went to Cerro Gorda, Tennessee.

William Thomas and Henry Brumley, the two brothers that fought for the confederacy, went back to Franklin County, Alabama. Life was not easy for the losers of this war. They had lost everything that they worked for. Years later both brothers went to prison for murder.

Everyone did not just lay down their guns after the war, especially in places like Franklin County, where there was so much mistrust and hatred. The Brumley's were known as God fearing people, but they were always armed and ready to fight back.

The brothers carried barlow knives. They trained some of the confederate soldiers to use a knife. They called it Indian fighting.

William Thomas was cut across his stomach. He killed the man, and was arrested for manslaughter. He was released because the other man started the fight.

After his first wife died, William Thomas married her sister, Martha Clement. In 1860, they settled on a farm near Hodges, Alabama. For twenty five years, they farmed their land, and raised their children. Although they lived a quiet life, a generation would pass before these soldiers could lay down their arms.

One day, William Thomas got in an argument with his neighbor. Some say it was over a land line, others say it was because of a cow. Whatever it was, it was trivial and happened all at once. He walked in his house and said, "I just killed the best friend I ever had".

After hiding out in the freedom hills for eighteen months, he was charged with murder. The law brought him to Tuscumbia, Alabama, to get him out of Franklin County. He died in 1890, at Wetumka Prison, after serving three years of a ten year sentence.

Sources:

Brumley story of amputation - told by Velma Montgomery-grand daughter of William Thomas Brumley

Fighting at Burnsville- Pinkney Hall- National Tribune Dec. 14, 1899

Henry Cagle - original land entries Walker Co. Ala. (#63) October 1836.

Charles Cagle - Heritage of Winston County, Alabama

CHAPTER 10

THE MARLAR - CUMMINGS - LAMBERT FAMILY

Marlene Bonds shared several stories about the Cummings family. The first to settle in Tishomingo County was Christopher (Doc) Cummings. The Cummings family was on their way to Arkansas. As they tried to cross a creek in Burnsville, their covered wagon got stuck and broke down. Doc found work cutting timber, so they decided to stay. His brother's family, whom they were traveling with, went on to Arkansas.

Doc was the first registered veterinarian in Tishomingo county. He raised his family in Pumpkin Center. A community east of Burnsville on the road to Iuka. Doc's mother taught people to read in Franklin County, Alabama. Their home town was Double Springs. Doc carried on the tradition. He had a table set up in the Burnsville Post Office. There he taught men to read and sign their name.

Cummings Geneology

Beverly Anne Cummings (1958-2011) (b. and d. Iuka, Ms.)
husband: Alvin Troy MarlarJr. (1953-2013) (b. and d. Burnsville, Ms.)

Arlander L. Cummings "Arlie" (1915-1990) (b. and d. Tishomingo Co. Ms.)
wife: Ruby Jewel Lambert (1916-1969)(b. and d. Tishomingo Co. Ms.)

Christopher Columbus "Doc" Cummings(1862-1938) (b. Ala. d. Burnsville, Ms.)
wife: Francis Hartley (1888-1935) (b. Tenn. d. Burnsville, Ms.)

William Frank Cummings (1835-1869) (b. South Carolina d. Winston, Ala.)
wife: Elmina Cagle (1838-1910) (b. Hardin, Tenn. d. Burnsville, Ms.)

Absolem Abner Cummings (1811-1886) (b. Rockingham, N.C. d. Mt. Pleasant, Maury, Tenn.)
wife: Nancy Wright (1814-1865) (b. South Carolina d. Winston, Ala.)

Josiah Cummings (1787-1840) (b. N.C. d. Alabama)
wife: Mary A. Young (1765-1820) (b. Rowan, N.C. d. Rockingham, N.C.)

Jacob Cromer (1733-1792) (b. Erpfingen, Reutlingen, Baden-Württemberg, Germany d. Newberry, S.C.)
wife: Elizabeth Yost (1740-1833) (b. and d. Newberry, S.C.)

Arley and Ruby Jewell Lambert Cummings

Lambert Genealogy

Ruby Jewel Lambert (1916-1969) (b. and d. Tishomingo Co. Ms.) husband: Arlander "Arlie" Cummings (1915-1990) (b. and d. Burnsville, Ms.

Daniel "Dan" Lambert (1880-1949) (b. and d. Burnsville, Ms.) wife: Mary Elizabeth Wren (b. McNairy, Tenn. d. Tishomingo Co. Ms.)

James Monroe Lambert (1845-1887) (b. and d. Burnsville, Ms.) wife: Tabitha Willis (1851-1908) (b. Hardin, Tenn. d. Burnsville, Ms.)

James Clyde "Jim" Lambert (1819-1869) (b. McNairy, Tenn. d. Burnsville, Ms.) wife: Lucretia Willis (1823-1906) (b. Morgan, Ala. d. Burnsville, Ms.)

John Lambert (1747-1803)(b. S.C. d. Burnsville, Ms.)
wife: Nancy Carpenter (1770-1855) (b. Rutherford, N.C, d. Tishomingo, Ms.)

The Marlar family

The first Marlar in our family to settle in Tishomingo County was Reuben Rufus Marlar.

Born in Kentucky in 1819,. He married Minerva Whitehead at age twenty. At the age of 26, he married Janette Reynolds in Tishomingo Co. Ms. 1845.

Rufus served in the civil war in the E 12 Tenn. Cavalry. He received a land grant in Tishomingo Co. for 160 acres (T25 R10E S8).

Rufus is buried at Frayley Chapel in Alcorn Co. Ms.

Children of Rufus and Nettie Marlar are:

Minerva Marlar 1846
George Marlar 1848-1923
Sarah Marlar 1851
James Marlar 1852
Rueben Marlar 1853-1927
John W. Marlar 1858-1944
Joseph Rubin Marlar 1861-1923
Thomas Franklin Marlar 1864-1947
Mary Mollie Marlar 1866

Joseph Rubin Marlar (Joe) moved from Alcorn County, to Tishomingo County in 1881 after he married Mary Lucinda Lambert (Mollie). They lived in Coles Mill until he died in 1923. Joe and Mollie Marlar are buried in Mulberry Cemetery near Coles Mill, Ms.

Children of Joe and Mollie Marlar are:
Bascomb Marlar 1882
James Monroe Marlar 1883-1954
Gay Marlar 1884
Coney Marlar 1885-1948
Rubin Kelse Marlar 1887-1951
Annie Pearl Marlar 1889-1967
Oscar Marlar 1892=1977
William Kimble Marlar 1893-1984
Kern Marlar 1894
Lular Annis Marlar 1897-1977
Early Earnest Marlar 1898-1916
Thomas Marlar 1900=1983
Paul Marlar 1902-1969
Silas Marlar 1904-1986
Charlie Buster Marlar 1905
Gladys Marlar 1908-1963

William Kimble Marlar (Kim) (1893-1984) Kim was born in Kendrick, Alcorn Co. Ms. His family moved to Coles Mill, tishomingo Co. Ms. before he was six years old. On 24 Sept. 1911, Kim Marlar married Addie Blakney (1896-1985)They lived at Coles Mill until 1930, when they moved to Burnsville, Ms. Addie and Kim had a family farm. Kim also worked in sawmills part of the year. One of the big government jobs he worked on was clearing yellow creek for a canal. It would later become the Tennessee Tombigbee Waterway, In 1940, Kim operated a service station in Burnsville. He also operated "The Victory Cafe" in Burnsville during World War II.

Addie and Kim Marlar had the following children:
William Floyd Marlar (1913)
Audie B. Marlar (1916-1984)
Alvin Troy Marlar Sr. (1922-1997)
Florence Marlar (1926)

Alvin Troy Marlar Sr. was born May 26, 1922. At age 24, Alvin married Ruby Louise Hubbard (1927-1990) on 14 Sept. 1946. They met at the train depot.

During the 1940's two passenger trains stopped in Burnsville two times a day. One in the morning the other in the afternoon. At midnight the express passenger train went through, but it did not stop. Many passengers loaded the trains at the Burnsville Depot. They often got off in Iuka in the morning and rode the train back in the afternoon. Corinth or Iuka was about as far as most people went.

The steam engine had to be filled with water at the Corinth Depot. It was a bigger depot. Two railroads crossed at Corinth, The Illinois Central and the Norfolk Southern.

The train also carried the mail. Sometimes there was a whole truck bed of mail. Especially during World War II. That's the only way of hearing from the soldiers. Families would wait all day to pick up a letter at the post office. They usually spent the whole day in town anyway because they did not come that often.

Girls would hang out by the train tracks when the troop trains came through. Soldiers would hang out the windows and wave at them. The girls wanted to give the boys a good send-off.

Dr. Montgomery was the local doctor. He delivered many babies. Edra Osborn said he delivered her husband, Billy Joe Osborn. He was supposed to deliver her, but the doctor did not get there in time. Maxie Seaton, their neighbor delivered her.

George Lambert remembers a trip to Dr. Montgomery's office, when he was a young man. a knot about the size of a dime, came up on his lip. Dr. Montgomery said, 'I am afraid to cut on that. I'll have to take you to Memphis." Doctor Montgomery had the fanciest car in town. Mable, his wife, had to drive it because the doctor had a peg leg.

George thought she drove too fast. That was his first time to ride in a car. He had never moved that fast. Memphis was the first city he had ever seen. Corinth was the furthest he had been from home.

Alvin had just returned from service in the army during World War II. The couple made Burnsville their home.

Alvin ran an Automobile Body Shop. He also taught at the Tishomingo Vocational Center. The couple raised their children in Burnsville. Both are buried at Harmony Hill Cemetery.

"The Rooster Fighter"

Alvin Marlar loved to help his neighbors. He had a very generous spirit, especially with the elderly.

On spring day, he brought his tractor to Esther Compton's house to break up her garden. When he finished, Miss Esther was waving from her porch. She wanted him to come pick up his pay. She said. "I don't dare get off this porch." On her leg were long bloody gashes. "There's a devil rooster that spurs me every time I go into the yard. I tried to shoot it, but I missed!"

Seeing that Miss Esther really needed his help, Alvin came up with a plan. He got a tow sack and a bushel basket out of her feed shed. While Alvin hid around the corner of the house, Esther walked out into the yard. The rooster was in the barnyard, when he spied her. Here he come, flapping his wings and ruffling his feathers. If that was meant to intimidate. It worked!

Esther took off running in the wrong direction. They were doing some fast zig zagging around that yard. Here comes Alvin sprinting up behind. He popped the basket over the rooster and lay down across it.

It took a long while before they got their breath. Alvin kept holding that basket down until Esther got a fishing net. With that they finally wrangled the rooster into the tow sack.

Esther said, "Just take that net with you!" She did not want to take the chance that the devil would get loose.

Alvin Marlar had a lot of jewels in his crown because of the many good deeds he did. He had many friends that loved him.

The children of Alvin and Louise Marlar are:
Nelta Marlar
Videnda Marlar
Alvin Troy Marlar Jr. (1953-2013)

Alvin Troy Marlar Jr. was born 19 June, 1953 to Alvin and Louise Marlar in Burnsville, Ms. He was a lifelong resident of Burnsville. He served as Mayor of the town in the 1970's. He had the distinction of being the youngest Mayor in Mississippi. AT as he was called, married Beverly Anne Cummings (1956-2011). They had one child, Alvin Troy Marlar III.

Alvin Troy Marlar Jr., Anne Cummings Marlar Little T

AT's second wife was Cindy Timbes. They had three children:

Justin Marlar
Josh Marlar
Brandy Marlar

The Lambert Family

Anne Cummings mother was Ruby Jewell Lambert. Her father was Arlie Cummings. Anne was only eleven years old when her mother died. Her brothers and sisters help raise her.

Grandmother Mary Lambert told about the first time she rode in an automobile. The family was enjoying a picnic under the trees at the Burnsville well. It was located on main street. It was full of people on Sunday afternoons. Doctor Harris bought a car. The first one they had seen. The horses that pulled their wagons did not like the noise it made. They would have run off if they weren't tied. For a nickel, the doctor would take you for a ride. Wow! it was so fast.

"The Lambert, Marlar Feud"

It is sad to say! My grandkids Great Grandpa, Joe Marlar killed their Great Grandpa, James Lambert.

There's been bad blood between the Lambert and Marlar families since the civil war. James Lambert and his brother were cutting timber. Joe Marlar came by with some whiskey. For some reason they got into a fight. James' brother tried to chop Joe with an axe. Later that week, a group of men were sitting under the trees by the city well. That was a favorite drinking spot. A big clap of thunder and a flash of lightening sent everyone to the store fronts just across the street.

Joe Marlar walked by and stabbed James Lambert in the gut. They laid him on a store counter and tried to pack the wound. Joe came in the store and asked what happened. James was alert enough to name him as the attacker.

Jame's wife and children watched as two men carried their Daddy on a homemade stretcher made out of a door they took off of a shed. They took him to his house. His wife said, "Kids, your Daddy is a dead man." James Monroe Lambert died a few days later.

James answered the alter call and repented of his sins the night before he was stabbed. He is buried in the Lambert family cemetery, which is also known as Possom Trot.

Marlar Genealogy

Alvin Troy Marlar Jr. (1953-2013) (b. and d. Burnsville, Tishomingo Ms.)
wife: Beverly Anne Cummings (1958-2011) (b. and d. Tishomingo, Ms.)

Alvin Troy Marlar Sr. (1922-1997) (b. and d. Burnsville, Tishomingo, Ms.)
wife: Ruby Louise Hubbard (1927-1990) (b. and d. Tishomingo, Ms.)

William Kimble "Kim" Marlar (1893-19840) (b. Kendrick, Ms. d. Burnsville, Tishomingo Ms.)
wife: Addie C. Blakney (1896-1985) (b. and d. Tishomingo, Ms.)

Joseph Rubin "Joe" Marlar (1861-1923) (b. and d. Tishomingo, Ms.)
wife: Genettie Reynolds (1822-1912) b. Tenn. d. Alcorn, Ms.)

Allen Rubin Marlar(1795-1830) (b. Va. d. Tenn.)
wife: Mary Polly Barnes (1790-1860) (b. Granville, N.C. d. Tishomingo, Ms.)

Reuben Benjamin Marlow (1750-1792) (b. Va. d. Edgecombe, N.C.)
wife: Ann Drake (1748-1799) (b. Va. d. N.C.)

John Marlow (1730-1824)

Hubbard genealogy

Ruby Louise Hubbard (1927-1990) (b. and d. Tishomingo, Ms.)
husband: Alvin Troy Marlar (1922-1997) (b. and d. Tishomingo, Ms.)

Eugene Augustus Hubbard (1905-1954) (b. Iuka, Tishomingo, Ms.
d. Los Angeles, California)
wife: Ruby Mae Williams (1908-1959) (b. Tenn.

John Breckenridge Hubbard Sr. (1860-1913) (b. Ms. d. Memphis,
Shelby, Tenn.)
wife: Annie Belle Dean (1860-1924) (b. and d. Ms.)

David Reeder Hubbard (1812-1889) (b. Pendleton, Anderson, S.C.
d. Iuka, Tishomingo, Ms.)
wife: Clarinda Millsaps (b. Cartersville, Bartow, Ga. d. Iuka,
Tishomingo, Ms.)

David Hubbard (1788-1879) (b. S.C. d. Iuka, Tishomingo, Ms.)
David was the founder of the town of Iuka.

"The Meanest Town in Mississippi"

Edra Lambert Osborn recalls Burnsville in the 1940's. Her family moved here, when she was nine years old. George Lambert, her dad bought the Victory Cafe from Kim Marlar. If you came up main street, on the left was the train tracks, a depot, and the city well.

On the right was a long line of businesses. Jack Timbes operated a cafe. with a pool hall in the back. His brother Kelly Timbes ran a barbershop in the same building. Next door was a theatre. A long glass front building held the Post Office. Miss Goldie Oaks was the post master. Luther Strickland ran a dry goods store.

Luther Kennedy owned most of the land in Burnsville. He did not own the businesses but he owned most of the buildings.

The Victory Cafe had a restaurant in the front, and a feed store in the back. The back of all the stores opened into an alley. Nine year old Edra, loved to sit at the front table and watch the trains go by.

There was one more store on the corner of this block. Buster Marlar operated a meat market in the front. Opening to the alley was a jail. That jail stayed full. Burnsville had a reputation for being a mean place. A lot of whiskey drinking took place here. Some say it was the meanest town in Mississippi. It had more than it's share of fighting, stabbing, and shooting.

One night, George was emptying the ice out of his drink boxes. A voice from the jail pleaded, "Give me some water." George took the man a drink and a hamburger.

Edra had a dog named Skipper. He was known as a mean dog. He would not let anyone in the alley look in their windows. One night, someone cut Skipper's throat. He was in the alley behind the store.

It cut him bad, but it did not kill him. He barked at a lot of people, but he especially hated one man. George kept Skipper, because he knew he would protect Edra.

Across the street, another block began. The Blakney's owned a store across from the city well. There was no space between the buildings, they joined each other. Fannie Collons Cafe, Bob Tucker Store, Bal Foote general store, and Charley Epperson's service station filled the block.

Across the street, Addie Marlar ran a cafe. If you wanted to know everything that happened in Burnsville, All you had to do was eat at Addie's.

Across the tracks from the city well once stood a hotel. Guests could walk from the depot to get a room.

Behind the alley, near the Baptist Church stood a cotton gin and a black smith's shop. Three colored families lived behind the gin. One of the old ladies lived to be over one hundred years old. She was a mid-wife. For years, she helped whoever needed her. These families were also known as whiskey makers.

George Lambert got an A Model automobile from Rast Hicks. One of the colored men had been beaten and left in the road. George picked the man up. He drove down the street, past the men who beat him, and took him home.

In those days a lot of people walked the roads. Sometimes George picked up tramps and soldiers. He often brought them home and fed them a good breakfast. He was also known to take drunks home. Most of them were his family.

Several big white houses stood on Eastport street. The Gober house stood where our bank is located today. Joe Myers, who was the mayor of Burnsville owned a house on the same street. Luther Kennedy, the richest man in Burnsville lived near the Baptist Church.

In the 40's Burnsville was the newest and most modern school in the county. The brick building had an auditorium with surrounding classrooms. When Edra was in fifth grade, she was in this building. Mr. Sheffield was her spelling teacher. He was also the principal. The whole fifth grade assembled on the stage of the auditorium. Mr Sheffield called out spelling words. If you missed a word you had to sit down.

The word "bouquet" wiped out most of the class. She was the only one left standing. The sixth grade came in. Edra spelled through their class. The word "refrigerator" wiped the last of the sixth graders out. Again she was the last one standing. Mr. Sheffield told her to come on down and go join your class.

Some of Edra's Burnsville teachers were Alton Marlar, Dorothy Garret, Cleston Scruggs, and Jim Cummings.

Burnsville School

Sources:

"Burnsville in the 40's" - story by Edra Lambert Osborn

Grand Mother Lambert- story by Marlene Bonds- grand daughter of Dan Lambert

Marlar Lambert Feud- story by Marlene Bonds

1880 US Census 2nd District Alcorn County, Ms.

1900, 1910, 1920, 1930 US Census Coles Mill, Tishomingo Co. Ms. district 0113

1940 US Census Burnsville, Tishomingo Co.

CHAPTER 11

THE WELCH FAMILY - EASTPORT

Jesse Welch was the first of the Welch family to come to Tishomingo County, Mississippi. Born in Greenville, South Carolina, he married Nancy Moore. Nancy and Jesse had the following children:

Jessie Bluford Welch (1835)
William C. Welch (1836)
Oliver Albert Welch (1837 - 1862)
Zadock Welch (1840)
Caroline Welch (1844 - 1932)

All of their children were born in Greenville, South Carolina.
In 1849 Jesse married Martha F. Houston (1831 - 1907) while living in Eastport, tishomingo county, Mississippi. Jesse and Martha had the following children.

James Daniel Welch (1850 - 1930)
Joseph Welch (1859 - 1942)
Adeline Delphia "Addie" Welch (1861 - 1894)
Jestana "Jessie Lee" Welch (1861)
John F. Welch (1864)
Robert Monroe Welch (1866 - 1888)
Albert Lee Welch 1869 - 1926)

Charles Thomas Welch (1875 - 1964)

The census of 1850 lists Jesse Welch's occupation as a grocery keeper in Eastport, Ms. He applied for a license to operate The Welch Saloon of Eastport in 1851 and each year until 1866. He also operated the Welch Wingo Saloon located in Iuka from 1857 through 1861.

In 1857 the maximum fee that a tavern owner could charge in Tishomingo County was:
(3 meals and lodging for 1 man, 3 feeds and lodging for a horse $2.00)
1 man per day $1.00
1horse per day $1.00
1 single meal 50 cents
1 single feed 50 cents
1 nights lodging 25 cents

Jessie moved to Savannah, Tennessee in 1870. In 1880 he was a farmer in Texas. Jesse died in 1895 and is buried in Stampede Valley, McLennan Texas.

Jesse' son Oliver Alberry Welch moved to Tishomingo County with his father from Greenville, South Carolina. At the age of twenty one, Oliver married Rosaline Ashley (1841 - 1906) on 25 February, 1858.

They had two children born in Eastport, Ms.
Julius Oliver Welch (1858-1935)
Annie O. Welch (1862-1932)

In 1860 Oliver, Rosaline, and the two children lived in the home of her father Preston Ashley. Preston was a boat engineer in Eastport, Ms.

Oliver was a casualty of the civil war in 1862. At this time, the couple's home was Eastport, Ms. It was also the year Eastport was under fire, during the civil war.

"The Gunboats"

Jeremiah Welch told about being fired on by gunboats. He was on the Tennessee River below the bluffs at Eastport. When they started firing at him, he slid off of his horse and headed for the bushes. They kept firing at him while he climbed the bluffs. Finally he got over the hill and out of their range. His white horse was climbing right up behind him. The Federals could see the white horse climbing, when they could not see the man.

Jeremiah made a crop each year on his mother's land. When he was not farming, he took the team of mares and wagon to visit his brother in Eastport. He went with his brother, who was a merchant to buy freight off the boats. On his way home, Jeremiah sold to merchants along the river. He started making regular stops at Neshoba, Cook's Landing, Hamburg, Pittsburg, and Crump Landing. He later expanded his trade to include the inland villages of Purdy, Kendrick, Glendale, Burnsville, Carrolville, and Danville. Hauling freight proved to be a profitable business.

In 1870, Rosaline and the two children were living in Bishop, Marshall County Kentucky. The family fled Eastport after it was occupied by the federals and her first husband was killed in 1862. They lived in the same house as her father and mother, Preston and Catherine Ashley.

On April 13, 1871 Rosaline married Calvin Thomas Bazzell (1835-1897) in Marshall County Kentucky. The couple moved back to Hardin County, Tennessee. They had three children born in Hardin County.

Robert Lee Bazzell (1872-1927)
Leona Bazzell (1875-1954)
Nellie B. Bazzell (1879-1961)

In 1880, Calvin, Rosaline, the Welch children, the Bazzell children, and grandmother Catherine all lived in Hardin County. Calvin was a blacksmith and twenty one year old Julius was a farmer.

Rosaline lived in Hardin County, Tn. until she died on 23 July 1906. She is buried in the Shanghai Cemetery near Counce, Tennessee.

Julius married Mary Louise Sawyer (1862-1915) on 24 December, 1882. Like Julius, Mary was born in Eastport. Ms.

In 1900, Julius Oliver Welch lived on the Red Sulfur Springs Road in Hardin. County. His wife Mary and their six children lived with him. Julius was the Post Master at the Red Sulfur Post Office. It was located in the Red Sulfur Hotel. Children of Julius and Mary Welch are:

William Julius Welch (1883-1974)
Mary R. Welch 1885-1915)
Maude Welch (1888-1966)
Seldon Welch (1890-1969)
Sallie Welch (1893-1984)
Clarence Welch (1896-1934)
Earnest Welch (1900-1990)
Leonard Welch (1904-1988)
Ruth Welch (1906-1911)

Julius died at age 76 in Hardin County, Tn. on April 25, 1935.

Clarence Welch married Era Irene Brown from Nixon, Hardin County, Tn.
Clarence and Era had the following children:

James Clarence Welch (1920-2005) wife: Rachel Mann Brumley
Mary Arbelle Welch (1923-2006) husband: Gene Layton
Ruth Irene Welch (1925 - 2013) husband: Charley Broadway
Daniel Sidney Welch (1927-2006) wife: Jean Cook

Era, Daniel, James, Ruth Welch and Tootsie Broadway

Clarence Welch was a Church of God preacher. He built a church at the top of Red Sulfur Hill in Hardin County. The family home was located just across the road from the church. After Clarence died, the home burned. Era and the Welch children moved into the church and converted it into a house.

Clarence was also an undertaker. His name appears on death certificates from Hardin County. He died at age thirty seven with Tuberculosis. Junior Welch said his Uncle Clarence contacted TB while he was in France during World War I.

Era had children ranging from age 9 to 14, when Clarence died. She supported them by taking in boarders. Many workers were in this area working on Pickwick Dam. Era furnished them a room. On a wood stove, she cooked their meals and washed their clothes. After years of work, Pickwick Dam was completed in 1937.

Sisters, Mary Arbell Welch Layton
Ruth Welch Broadway

Our family's Welch Genealogy

James Clarence Welch (1920-2005) born: Red Sulfur, Hardin Co. Tn. wife; Rachel Mann Brumley (1933-2018) born: Short, Ms. Both are buried at Hubbard Salem Cemetery

Clarence Welch (1896-1934) born: Counce, Hardin Co. Tn. wife: Era Irene Brown (1902-1971) Both are buried at Shanghai Cemetery.

Julius Oliver Welch (1858-1935) born: Eastport, Ms. wife: Mary Louise Sawyer (1862-1915) born: Eastport, Ms. buried Shangai Cemetery, Hardin Co. Tn.

Oliver Alberry Welch (1837-1862) born Greenville, SC. lived at Eastport, Ms. in 1860 wife: Rosalie Ashley (1841-1906) born: Kentucky died Hardin Co. Tn. buried at Shanghai Cemetery

Jesse Welch (1813-1895) born Greenville, SC, lived at Eastport, Ms, Counce, Tn., Savannah Tn, McLennan, Texas. 1st wife: Nancy

Moore (1814-1844) 2nd wife: Martha F. Houston (1831-1907) Jesse and Martha are buried in Stampede Valley, Texas.

Brown Genealogy

Era Inez Brown (1902-1971) (b. Nixon, Hardin, Tn. d. Counce, Hardin, Tn.)
1st husband: Clarence Welch(1896-1934) (b. Tn. d. Counce, Hardin, Tn.)
2nd husband: Charlie Chamblis Worley (Jaunce)

Franklin Marion Brown (1883-1924) ((b. Hardin, Tn d. Longview, Oktibbeha, Ms.)
wife: Lulia Arbel Duncan (1879-1917) (b. and d. Hardin, Tn.)

Roland H. Brown (1859-1918) (b. Carlockville, Tn. d. Greenville, Green, Tn.)
wife: Mary "Mollie" Elizabeth Kilpatrick (1858-1928) (b. and d. Savannah, Hardin, Tn.)

Sources:

Fan Cockron, History of old Tishomingo County 102,109,119,122, 126,128,132,141,144,173,228,242,1850 Census Eastport, Ms.

1860 Census Eastport, Tishomingo Co. Ms.
1870 Census Marshall County, Kentucky1880
1900 - 1910 Census Hardin County, Tn.

Sargent James C. Welch   James and Rachel Welch

James enlisted in the army on 10 Sept. 1941 and served until 24 Dec. 1945.

He served in Company D, 771st tank division in the Battle of the Bulge with General Patton.

I never heard him talk about his time in the war. Once Mom was telling someone he was a paratrooper. He quickly corrected her, "All of the tank soldiers were air lifted. We had to jump out of the plane with a parachute. That's how they got us to the front lines where our tanks were waiting." "We jumped, but we were not paratroopers". Mom quickly changed the subject.

At Home in Iuka

Rachel Brumley bought two and a half acres of land from Mr. Johnny Woodruff. It was located on West Ash Street in Iuka. She hired Hershel Brown, a local carpenter to build her house. Rachel and her four children moved there in 1958. Her neighbors were Clifford and Emma Rast, Frank and Mae Brown, and Mrs. Katie Horn.

Just up the road, Charley and Ruth Broadway were building a new house. Until they got their well dug, drinking water had to be carried from the neighbor's well. Rachel knew Ruth. They worked together at the shoe factory. Ruth's brother, James Welch, was helping build the house. That's how Rachel and James got acquainted. He came after water. I think there was a little match-making going on. They got married in February of 1960. Here they raised four children: Betty, Nelda, Shirley, and Stanley Brumley. The house on Ash Street was their home for over 50 years. They lived here until their death in 2005 and 2018.

"The Thanksgiving Squirrel"

Rachel and James enjoyed the holidays with their family. Their house was always filled with sixty people every Thanksgiving and Christmas. Food was everywhere. The rooms were small, but they always held a few more each year. As the children moved out with families of their own, they took turns hosting Thanksgiving. There was only one place we could have Christmas. It had to be at the Welch house.

We always put up the Christmas tree on Thanksgiving Day. Most houses built in the sixties were small. There was not any room for storage. The Christmas tree was placed in a box, securely taped, and stored in an outside shed until the next year.

Outside storage caused some unforeseen excitement. The crowd left, dishes were washed and all that turkey was put away. A couple teenagers stayed to decorate the tree. One of the young men got the tree out of the shed and placed it in the living room.

The girls could not wait to open that box. They pulled the tape off, expecting to see that beautiful tree. Two beady eyes looked up at them.

The girl's blood curling screams put that box into motion. A squirrel shot out. Up the curtains, around the room, down the hall. It would be hard to say who was the craziest, the squirrel or the kids. Both went berserk!

All at once the trauma ceased. The squirrel was hiding under the bed. "What's our plan?" "Close the inside doors!. Open the outside doors! Let it run out!"

That squirrel ran past the open door and hid in the kitchen. It was stuck to the top of the cabinets. Casey, the bravest said, "I will take the broom and swish it toward the door."

"Everybody stand back! Don't scare it!

When she moved that broom, It must have spied an escape plan. Down the handle it shot, up Casey's arm, over the shoulder, and down her back.

"Get it off!!   Get it off!!

By the time she got the words out the squirrel was gone. But that did not stop her from trying to rid herself of that critter.

She was jumping in the air and rolling on the floor. Everyone, including the squirrel, was heading for the back door.

I have a hard belly laugh each year, when my Christmas tree is pulled out of it's box. My grand kids wonder what's so funny about a Christmas Tree!

During the 60's, James and Rachel usually crossed the state line every Sunday. The family loved to visit James' mother, Era, and her 2nd husband, Jaunce Worley who lived at the top of Red Sulfur Hill in Hardin County.

Our grandfather Worley was raised in the Pyburn Community, just north of Pickwick Dam. He lived at Pickwick before the dam was built in 1957. As children, he would amaze us with stories about the River. He worked at the Pickwick Marina. We spent many days swimming at Pickwick circle. A few times we rented a boat from the marina.

Jaunce heard a lot of fish tales. Fish photos filled the walls of the marina. Some were as tall as we were. He told us there were catfish in that river that could swallow us in one gulp. We did not believe him, but it kept us close to the bank while swimming.

Grandma Worley was known for her good cooking. She often cooked with duck eggs. Their yard was full of chickens and green headed ducks. These mallards are usually not tame ducks. Once a nest, by the marina, was disturbed by a boat.

Jaunce rescued the eggs and placed them under his setting hens. Three ducks hatched. It was so funny to watch the frustrated hens. The baby ducks swam in their water bowls. Since that worked, Pa Worley raised a few ducks each spring.

Pa Worley knew all about the river and the animals that lived there. He could name all the different boats, barges, trees, birds, and snakes. He also knew a lot of history about the river. I can hear him saying, "Now, this is how the Indians lived and used the river. If a snake swims on top of the water it is probably poison. If it swims under water and sticks it's head up, it is not poison.

"Charley, the Catfish"

There was one fish tale I questioned. Although if Pa Worley said it happened that way, it probably did.

He had a small trot line, he threw out once a week. Maw Worley liked for him to bring fresh fish home. One day he caught a catfish that was 2 feet long. He put it in a 5 gallon bucket with a little water in it. It stayed there most of the day. The marina was busy and he did not go to clean the fish until later that afternoon. "Well, I guess Era will not eat fish tonight." The bucket was turned over and the fish was gone. He thought it probably flopped back into the water.

A couple days later, a sliding sound came from under the minnow vat. Checking out the sound, Pa Worley looked in the mouth of that big old catfish. Wondering, How is that fish still alive? It was damp where he was hiding, but the fish was not submerged in water. It's gills and mouth were moving.

Pa tossed it a piece of old cheese. That fish swallowed the cheese. "I'll come back later and drag it out with my fishing pole." Then he thought, "I don't know about eating a fish that should have been dead three days ago. A month passed by. The fish became "Charley". It would actually come up and eat the cheese from Pa Worley's hand.

On the fourth of July speed boats roared their powerful engines. Crowds filled the park at Pickwick Circle. It was the day for boat races at Pickwick. That was the last time Pa Worley saw Charley the Catfish. He wondered if he would drown if he went back into the water. Charley never came back to the marina. Pa suspected he did not like all the noise caused by the racing boats.

During the 1960's, Our family rode a ferry across the Tennessee River. It crossed just below the Pickwick Dam, at the boat ramp. On one of our trips, we watched an older man drive upon the boat and go right off the end of it. Lucky for him, a young man dove into the water and helped him get back to shore. We watched as an ambulance took the man to the hospital in Savannah. A wrecker pulled the car out of the river. We did not make it to church that Sunday.

We often went to church in Savannah and came back to Ma and Pa Worley's. The family liked to gather at their house for Sunday dinner and a few hours of visiting. On a few of these family gatherings, they made music. James's sister, Ruth Broadway and her husband Charley, played the guitar. They would play and sing and the whole family would join in.

Uncle Daniel's family played different instruments. One of my fondest memories of him is playing gospel songs on the accordion. James's favorite contribution was playing, "The Orange Blossom Special" on a harmonica. They did not do solo's, Everybody joined in the singing. We had so much fun! Maw Worley said, "Sing and make a joyful sound unto the Lord". Their songs were the most beautiful praise, I have ever heard.

James worked as a truck driver. He worked for Buster Ramsey Trucking in Iuka and the Fields brothers in Tennessee. For years he worked on 72 hwy from Memphis to Little Rock. That's when hwy 72 became a four lane road. As James got older shrapnel wounds in his back and legs caused him problems. Hip replacements forced him to retire from driving.

"The Trotline"

One of the things he liked to do after retirement was fish. That was his favorite pastime, until the day came that changed his life.

He loved to fish for Crappy in the early spring. One of the local fish markets told him they would buy all of the catfish he brought them. He put out a trotline to catch catfish. That went well for a while. Mostly he fished Bear Creek. After hearing channel catfish were biting near Colbert Landing. James decided to put a trotline in that part of the Tennessee River.

While running that trotline, his boat hit something in the water. It knocked the motor loose and burst the end out of his fiberglass boat. His weight was sinking the boat. Luckily, an island was not far away. He quickly took off all of his clothes and put on a vest lifejacket. James jumped into the water and towed his boat with the rope he used to tie off the boat. He managed to get to the island before the boat sank.

The first thing he did when he got to the island was put on his dry clothes and build a fire. He hoped it would lead rescuers to him. Because the boat did not sink, he had several essentials: A lighter, flashlight, dry coat, and some food. There was a knife and several tools in his tackle box.

This was before the days of cellphones. There was no way to call for help. Hoping to get the attention of a passing boat, He tied garbage bags to fishing poles. Just in case he could wave them in.

James was fairly comfortable sitting by a fire eating vienna sausages and crackers. He burnt his boat seat and all of the driftwood he could find. He thought he would probably be home before dark. A pile of wood was saved to burn at night, just in case he was still here.

Rachel would not miss him until after four, because he seldom came home before that time. No passing boats came close to him. He looked at the western sky and it was a wall of dark clouds.

Before the rain started, James pulled his boat as far as he could get it on the island. The cooler held one side up a couple feet. He had several life jackets that made a bed under the boat. When the rain started. He crawled into his shelter. It was going to be dark without a fire. The cord of his flashlight was wrapped around his arm. He knew he had to use it sparingly or the batteries would go down. He had to keep his lighter and flashlight dry. The wind hurled sprays of river water all the way to his boat. Thunder rolled and lightening flashed for hours.

Rachel reported James missing. They checked the boat dock to see if his vehicle was still there. Normally the rescue squad would have gone out when they saw he never returned to his vehicle. They could not go out until the next day, if the storm was over.

Rachel's neighbors and her parents sat with her all night. No one slept. No one believed he could have survived this storm. The preacher came and prayed with the family.

It was after dinner the next day before the storm ceased. Some of his fishing buddies led the rescue squad to the area where he was fishing. James was not able to call for help. They saw his boat.

After they got him to shore an ambulance took him to the hospital. He was cold, wet, and in shock. After a few days, he got out of the hospital and came home. As far as I know, That was the last time he fished the Tennessee River. The whole family was very thankful that he was still alive.

James started another hobby after he quit fishing. He loved to work in his wood shop. At first he made bird houses, picture frames, and art work. Demand for his products really picked up when he made porch swings and fish traps. That kept him busy for years.

Source

The tales of Jaunce Worley are the childhood memories of Betty Compton.
Stories of James Welch - childhood memories of Betty Compton
Jessie Welch Eastport— "The History of old Tishomingo County"
Story of Era Welch - Grandson, Jim Welch
Sargent James Welch - Fold 3

CHAPTER 12

RESEARCHING YOUR ROOTS

Traveling to an old home place is also a visit into the past. For just a little while, you walk the same paths, and see the same sights as the people that once lived here.

During the past five years, my mother and I have visited home places in the following locations:

Alabama - (Marion Co). Pikesville, (Winston Co.) Houston
Tennessee - (Hardin County) Savannah, Olive Hill, Holland Creek, Jonesboro
Georgia - (Pauling Co.)- Dallas, (Cherokee Co.)-Centre, (Gwinnett Co.) (Columbia Co.)
North Carolina - Ashville, Stantonville
South Carolina - Laurens, Newberry, Saluda
Virginia - Jamestown, Henrico
Massachusetts - Essex, Craigshead
Pennsylvania - Chester County
Maryland - Nottingham
Ruins of Crawford Castle - Kilbirnie, Scotland
England - London, Yorkshire

I have a few tips that might help, if you are trying to locate an old home place. Get a copy of the deed or land grant. Go to the County Court house where the homestead is located. They have a plat map of the county hanging on the wall. You can pin point the exact location by using the Township, Range, and Section numbers.

Find the names of roads you will take. Map out you trip. The names of many old roads are not on modern maps. They may not show up on a GPS. Many of these locations are off of the main road. They are covered with underbrush. I wear boots. Winter is the best time to explore because of snakes.

You can not always rely on cell phone reception. I like to take a compass with me. It is easy to get lost if there are no markers around. Always take a buddy with you. Be ready to defend yourself. You never know when you'll come across a wild animal.

Do not make yourself vulnerable to crime. Many of the older home sites are on unpopulated government land. If you drive for miles without seeing any one, and go to places called Cocaine Hollow. Realize you may not be safe.

Never go on private property without permission. If you can find a phone number it is best to call. If you can't call, Go to their house and ask permission. I have found many people were glad to share the information, and showed me historical sites. Others were hesitant. If that's the case, just walk away. Don't be persistent. There may be a reason you do not need to be there.

Once I drove up a dead end road. I read "No trespassing". I kept going because the road was narrow, and there was no place to turn around. At the end of the road, a house stood in a yard full of game chickens. On the front porch waved a six foot flag with a rattlesnake, "Don't tread on me". A big sign under the mailbox read, "Get out of the car, if you are ready to meet your maker". Needless to saw, I did not knock on that door.

It's getting harder to find signs of early settlers. In populated areas, civilization has taken over. Land is leveled and subdivisions occupy the spots where many settlements began. In Lilburn, Georgia, I found the parcel of land an ancestor lived on. There were three graves in the back yard of a subdivision. Daughters of the American Revolution (DAR) had placed a marker on the grave of a Revolutionary Soldier.

Many of the old family cemeteries do not have marked graves. They may have a rock, or at one time they may have had a wooden marker. Graves disappear when there's no family left to keep them up.

"The Hillbilly Spa"

On another ancestry trip, My mother and I drove to the site of a land grant that her great grandfather had gotten from the 1820 land lottery.

We stopped for breakfast at a little cafe. Across the road, a sign pointing up the mountain read, "Hillbilly Spa". The small restaurant was full. There was one table empty near the back door. A man with a long white beard and overhauls sat across from us. He said," The special is good here, I bring my own eggs."

"Can I interest you ladies in a massage at the Hillbilly Spa? It's the best rub down you'll ever get." He went on to describe his spectacular facility. I do my best work with mineral oil on a cedar coffin.

"I know just how to please the ladies. After I rub my hens, they just lay, lay, lay!" My Momma jumped up and said, "Let's Go!" As we got in the car she said, "That old codger needs to be castrated."

Historical Societies and Archives are very helpful. You need to call and make an appointment to visit them. They don't always keep regular hours. If you can give them family names, they will gather all the information they have.

Many have volunteers that can help you. Most are available by e mail. This is helpful if you are looking for specific information. Other times you just need to browse. You never know when you will find relevant information.

The Daughters of the American Revolution (DAR) have records of Revolutionary War Soldiers. I found their information very helpful, since most of the early settlers in South Carolina and northern Georgia moved there to get land grants. They were soldiers in the Revolutionary War. Most of the land grants in Alabama, came from soldiers that fought in the War of 1812.

My Mom and I visited the town of Crawford, Georgia. It was named after many of her relatives. That town has become a popular spot. Many scenes from "The Walking Dead" were filmed there. We also saw some of the old plantations.

I really wanted to visit Appling, Georgia, which was the home one of the original Columbia County settlers. We traveled down a dirt road to a town with dilapidated buildings and a very ornate, two story brick courthouse. A man from the Appling Historical Society met us at the old Columbia County Courthouse. It was built in 1812.

The land on which it stood was donated by Captain Charles Crawford. His home, located across the road from the court house, had burned years ago. The man took us on a tour of the court house. We saw the steps where Charles Crawford's son was killed by Indians, during an attack on the the early settlers.

Burial sites give a lot of information about a family. Early settlers buried their love ones near their home. Settlements had to be large enough to build churches before cemeteries were established. If there are no marked graves in cemeteries, old home places are the next place you need to look.

If the homesite is on private property, I usually do not ask to search for graves. A lot of people think you are looking for money. They don't want you digging up their property. Many are suspicious of the methods you use!

"Dousing for Graves"

Once a guide took my brother and I, to an old home site on his property. I asked if I could search for graves. I knew I would not be back there without him. He said," Look around, but I have not seen any markers." He pointed out where the house, barn, and out buildings stood.

The man looked a little perplexed when I took my dousing rods out of the trunk of the car. They were not elaborate equipment. I do not use them enough to buy expensive metal detectors. Two wire coat hangers are straitened, with six inches of the rod turned down to form a handle.

When you hold them over the grave of a male, both rods cross in an x shape. If you hold them over the grave of a female, the rods turn sharply to the right. The man followed me around the yard. If there is an old tree on the property, that's the first place I look. I found the grave of a man, a woman, and a small boy. A tent stake was placed at the points where the rods move. This shows the length of the grave.

The man said, "How did you do that? Do you have some kind of powers?" I think he thought I was a witch.

I was also a sceptic of this procedure, when I heard about "Dousing for Graves" at a Genealogy Fair. A lady named Chris, from an Alabama Historical Society was paid to flag unmarked graves in the city cemeteries. She showed her tools, and taught us to use them.

I tried the rods on marked graves in a cemetery. Later I tried them on an unmarked grave in the woods. They indicated a male or female consistently. Of course, I don't have a way of proving I have found a body. I am not going to dig them up. I do not know how it works? I suspect the metal detects minerals or some kind of energy in a body. I have tried it on old and new graves. Age does not seem to make a difference.

Once a man called. He wanted to hire me to find a grave. I told him I was not good enough to charge a fee. I had only done this a few times. It was a good tool to help with my research, but I did not claim to be a professional Douser.

He said, "Maybe you can give me an idea of where to dig". The man was the property owner. So, I knew it was legal to dig there. I told him I would help.

An old man lived on this property during the civil war. It was rumored that he acquired a large sum of money after his wife died. He took his money in coins. That kind of money would not rot. The old man did not trust banks. He did not tell anyone where his money was buried. There was no one he trusted with that information.

While riding home one night, the old man was shot and killed. He did not leave any directions to his money.

Since the old man's wife did not have a marked grave. The property owner thought she might be buried at the home place. It was common to bury valuables near a permanent marker. The money may have been hidden on her grave.

Slowly I walked over the entire yard, with outstretched dousing rods. I did not find the old man's wife. Those rods did not even detect an animal's grave. After I left, the man rented a backhoe.

Sources

My greatest source of information was my eighty year old mother, Rachel Welch. There was not a day in which she did not tell me some little tidbit of her life. If she could not give me the information I needed, she knew someone who could. Nothing brought her more joy than reminiscing the days of her youth.

Visiting the elderly, is something I will always cherish. So much knowledge and experience is lost with the passing of these beautiful souls.

It is an accomplishment to finish a project that I have worked on for five years. Even though I cannot force myself to write the words "The End".

The greatest reward is not the finished product. It is the people I met while putting this book together.

I dedicate this book to my Mother, Rachel Welch. Every day she reminded me to be proud of who I was, and where I came from!

Printed in the United States
By Bookmasters